"*The Only Certain Freedom* is a compelling and profound book about redemption in how we relate to work and the struggle to create something new in the world. Patrick O'Neill brings the power of mythology to life, his life and ours, which gives the book not only a certain freedom, but a certain depth. It is also gracefully written and thankfully absent of simplistic lists of steps to make your life better. The book is about the real hero's journey: Patrick has taken that journey both in his life/work and in the way he has written this book."

PETER BLOCK, author of *Flawless Consulting: A Guide to Getting Your Expertise Used*

"A truth-seeker and sage for the ages, Patrick O'Neill abandoned his comfortable but personally unsatisfying corporate job to pursue his growing interest in helping others realize their leadership potential. In the process, he changed his own life and the lives of countless others. *The Only Certain Freedom* is a must-read for all those who have ever contemplated bold career moves at any age, as well as for those searching to infuse more passion and purpose into their lives. As O'Neill artfully and expertly argues, it is possible to jump from a mundane to a meaningful path by tapping into the courage and conviction we all possess."

DR. SAMANTHA NUTT, bestselling author and founder of War Child Canada and USA

"I have personal experience with Patrick O'Neill, gained through the extraordinary work he did with me and my senior leadership from three different companies. Patrick is a gifted teacher and transformational consultant. His book *The Only Certain Freedom* is a must-read for entrepreneurs or those considering starting their own business. The book is full of valuable insights but also weaves Patrick's personal story through the narrative in a highly engaging style. Patrick is incredibly well read, and his quotes and insights from an eclectic range of thought leaders are joyful. The story is well crafted, well told, and well worth the read. Thanks, Patrick, for bringing this book to the innovators and dreamers who have the courage to start their own business on their own terms."

PAUL ALOFS, author of *Passion Capital: The World's Most Valuable Asset*

"An inspiring story of a modern man on a contemporary hero's journey to recover his soul and wake up fully to life. This book encourages us both professionally and personally to risk daily, forgive constantly, and remember that we are more than the habitual stories that have limited our choices."

FRANK OSTASESKI, author of *The Five Invitations: Discovering What Death Can Teach Us about Living Fully*

"The heroes who start a new business confront a 50 percent failure rate. Patrick O'Neill provides the essential guide for your quest in this thoroughly engaging book. O'Neill shows you how to avoid becoming a failure statistic through the skillful use of myth and with his personal story. Don't start a new business without reading this book."

DICK AND EMILY AXELROD, co-authors of *Let's Stop Meeting Like This: Tools to Save Time and Get More Done*

"Patrick is truly gifted in helping people transcend their ego. By sharing his own story of this, he inspires you to do the same— to let go of ego and instead use insightful introspection to help move you towards your own inspired purpose."

JILL NYKOLIATION, president of Juniper Park\TBWA

THE ONLY CERTAIN FREEDOM

THE ONLY

PATRICK O'NEILL

CERTAIN FREEDOM

THE TRANSFORMATIVE JOURNEY OF THE ENTREPRENEUR

THUNDER
MOUNTAIN

Thunder Mountain
www.extraordinaryconversations.com
Toronto ON
ISBN 978-1-7751722-0-8 (paperback)
ISBN 978-1-7751722-1-5 (ebook)

Produced by Page Two
www.pagetwostrategies.com
Cover and interior design by Peter Cocking and Taysia Louie
Printed and bound by Island Blue

17 18 19 20 21 5 4 3 2 1

The only certain freedom's in departure.

ROBERT FROST, "HOW HARD IT IS TO KEEP FROM BEING
KING WHEN IT'S IN YOU AND IN THE SITUATION"

For Lynne Stafford O'Neill

Contents

Acknowledgments

THIS BOOK was made possible by two forces: intuition and hard labor. When I first started writing, I was asked repeatedly by my friends what the book was about. For a perilously long time I didn't really know. Slowly it began to take shape. Some days, it felt as if I was building a house by hand with no architectural drawings. Other days, it was as if my hand was being directed by an unseen force. I cannot say the process was always easy or fun.

Unlike some people, for whom I carry an unhealthy envy, I am a slow writer. So the five years it took to finish the manuscript seemed a long time spent in the belly of the whale. Jonah was released in three days; I needed more time to marinate.

Unlike Jonah, however, I was not alone in this process. I had some very good companions, chief among them my editor, Tobin O'Donnell. Tobin provided a master class in writing. Patient and precise, Tobin was able to offer critical feedback that not only improved my writing but also encouraged me to stay the course over the years it took to reach my goal. All done with good humor, compassion, and when necessary, a firm hand. Thank you. You taught me to write the spare sentences of the heart.

Before her death in 2014, my friend and mentor Angeles Arrien offered valuable advice, especially about mythology. A protégée of Joseph Campbell and a cultural anthropologist by training, Angeles was instrumental in helping me understand how myth forms a hidden map of meaning that still guides us today. We led workshops together for twenty years, and through osmosis, I gained knowledge and insights that are represented on these pages.

I first read *Zen and the Art of Motorcycle Maintenance* by Robert Pirsig when I was eighteen. I found it in the bottom drawer of the book cabinet (a two-drawer affair) in the Hudson's Bay store in Lynn Lake, Manitoba. I was working in a nickel mine at the time. That store didn't offer much to a teenager: some Harlequin romances, children's stories, and bird guides. But there, at the bottom of a pile of stuff, was Pirsig's book. It inspired a lifelong love of inquiry and introduced me to the combination of storytelling and exposition that made *The Only Certain Freedom* possible.

Professor Ron Wareham taught Myths and Ideas at Concordia University, where I was a student in the 1970s. He first introduced me to the work of Joseph Campbell, Robertson Davies, and John Milton, among others. Myths and Ideas captured my imagination and enchanted my life. That class was the reason I stayed in school. I wish he were alive today to see how a seed he planted in uncultivated soil could produce a reasonable harvest.

Elinor Trainer has been a coconspirator for thirty-five years. She figures large in this story. I am grateful beyond measure for her friendship, good humor, and advice. She was instrumental in helping me remember some of the pivotal events of our shared history, and she also helped get the manuscript into shape. If God is in the details, then God is in constant touch with Elinor.

Grant McDiarmaid was instrumental in the development of Extraordinary Conversations. His support in the early years made a huge impact on me, my family, and the work. Thank you, Grant. You are a visionary.

Martin Rutte was an early mentor. He inspired me to set a goal for myself and pursue it no matter the difficulty. Reinhold

Schieber provided a safe harbor while I was "between the worlds" and lent moral and material support while I was setting up my business. Dan Ryan helped me understand that dreams require plans and budgets if they are to manifest.

Thank you to Carolyn Acker, Louis Rosenbaum, Tarianne DeYonker, Deborah Goldblatt, Arieahn Matamonasa Bennett, Neil Sawers, and Alannah O'Neill. They provided excellent feedback on early drafts of the manuscript and helped me make the writing more compelling and accessible to the reader.

Beth Nauman-Montana of Salmon Bay Indexing did the forensic work required to help a somewhat sloppy author construct the bibliography and footnotes.

The team at Page Two Strategies—Jesse Finkelstein, Amanda Lewis, Zoe Grams, Peter Cocking, and Eva van Emden—guided me every step of the way through the process of design, production, distribution, and marketing. They did so with an uncommon commitment to my vision for the book as well as for the reader's experience.

Thank you to the three beauties: my daughters, Alannah, April, and Ariana O'Neill. Much love and respect to the good people you have become. You take after your mother, the luminous Lynne Stafford O'Neill, to whom this book is dedicated.

Introduction

And there is no trade or employment but the young

man following it may become a hero.

WALT WHITMAN, *LEAVES OF GRASS*

ACCORDING TO the Global Entrepreneurship Monitor, there are approximately fifty million business start-ups around the world every year—more than a hundred thousand every day—and 300 million people taking a new product or service to market. Starting a business may appear on the surface to be a common undertaking, deeply rooted in the mud and brick of commercial markets. At its heart, though, launching a new business venture is more mythic than routine. Every year, people just like you and me do the heroic thing and set off on a journey into the unknown. More than half will fail. But, risk be damned, entrepreneurs have been seized by a dream (or are driven by a nightmare) that compels them forward.

This is the terra incognita of new enterprise. Here, like pilgrims, people survive by their wits, courage, resourcefulness . . . and, perhaps most importantly, by their faith.

Every entrepreneur is a dreamer. The desire to remake the world, or some small part of it, calls us from the "cubicle hell" to the threshold of adventure. This departure from the status quo, this appetite for freedom, is the hero's quest. In his book *The Hero with a Thousand Faces*, Joseph Campbell describes it as the "monomyth":

> A hero ventures forth from the world of common day into a region of supernatural wonder . . . fabulous forces are there encountered and a decisive victory is won . . . the hero comes back from this mysterious adventure with the power to bestow boons on his fellow man.[1]

The "region of supernatural wonder" is, perhaps, a little grandiose from the perspective of a newly minted entrepreneur. But let's look a little deeper. Like all heroes, entrepreneurs break with convention. They make a conscious decision to leave the comforts of a routine job and risk the uncertainties of a start-up business, or to leave the hothouse atmosphere and antiseptic case studies of business school and enter the cutthroat arena of economic survival, where they will be challenged from all sides.

You must ask yourself: Will my business model hold water? Do people want what I'm offering? Are my competitors doing it better? Is anyone listening? Can I handle the rigors of the entrepreneurial life—the long days; the sleepless nights; the fear, anxiety, and doubt?

Like every journey worth taking, starting a business is filled with joys and terrors, tests and treasures. On the way, we encounter angels, demons, and bankers—sometimes one and the same. This is not the easy way to make a living. It is a road of trials. There are no guarantees, no safety net should we fail. Nor is there a clock to punch, a boss to curry favor with, or a 401(k) to depend upon. Your thirst for success must be unquenchable; your willingness to work cannot be confined to eight-hour days. You are always immersed in problem solving, even when you sleep—if you sleep.

The boon you seek and the boon you find may not be the same. Fortune isn't always measured by success and wealth. What the entrepreneur is really searching for, through the medium of a start-up, is their best self. For those with an adventurous spirit, that best self can only be discovered in the death of the employee identity and—through the gristmill of mythic ordeals—the rebirth as an entrepreneur. As writer Jean Houston puts it:

> Many of us live on the surface of our lives, out of a very diminished and reduced notion of who and what we are, where we're going, what we can become. Myth is the remedy to this. Myth patterns the possibility of our larger story. It provides us with a domain of experience that our little, local lives have not provided. Myth gives us routes that we can take toward this larger life. Because we are storied and mythic, we can reenchant the world.[2]

Many entrepreneurial ventures do not survive this labyrinth of uncertainty. Success demands that you abandon the status quo and follow your heart. Each step is revealed, or concealed, by the previous step. A foot placed well gives you the traction you need to advance. A misstep has the potential to pitch you off the track.

Will you trust yourself? Will you have the guts to put everything on the line again and again? These are the quintessential questions every entrepreneur must answer. Self-sufficiency—the sum total of your knowledge, skill, courage, and resourcefulness—must buttress you against your competitors. Creative tension is implicit in this struggle, one that you must embrace to give birth to something new.

This book explores these questions through a binary structure of narrative and myth. The narrative is based on my own journey—events that occurred from 1987 to 1988, when I broke free from a career that made me profoundly unhappy and launched my own business. The myths that support the narrative attempt to uncover the hero's journey unfolding in what Houston refers to as "a little, local life."

Why explore myth in the context of modern enterprise? What could those hoary old stories reveal to us in our materialistic postmodern world?

A whole lot, I would argue. We are not the first people to set out in search of our destiny, and wisdom is a not a new invention. The old stories carry a set of hidden instructions to almost every modern quandary—how to live in the face of great challenges, what to do when you lose your way, how to discern what is most meaningful, how to meet gain and loss, and what constitutes true success. The answers are already there, waiting to be decoded. To break the code, we must understand the symbolic language of myth. This understanding can keep you sure-footed, able to pivot as necessary, guided by the hard-won wisdom of our prehistory. Why set out on such an adventure without a map?

I didn't know I was beginning a mythic journey when I started. Success was what I sought—success by my own definition and on my own terms. Whether you're like me and are simply seeking freedom and personal growth, or whether you have plans to disrupt the world through innovation, you are bound to retrace the hero's journey.

This can only happen when you answer the call to adventure. You will no longer be the hired hand working the decks of someone else's vessel. You'll captain the wheelhouse, in charge of your destiny. Cultural anthropologist and author Angeles Arrien says it well: "To reach the end of one's life and to know that one has not truly taken the journey or made a contribution is more terrible than any terrors one would have had to face on the way."

The products or services offered by entrepreneurs—the victor's spoils in the battle with the status quo—often bestow boons on the greater society. Think of the world after the Apple 1, Napster, Facebook, and the open-source movement, and that's just the technology sector. These were products of entrepreneurial fever dreams. They re-created the way the world works, and how we engage it. In doing so, your own life becomes re-enchanted.

The hero's journey is always there, lurking in the unconscious mind, waiting to be lived through us again. We are, all of us, Jonah and Theseus; Midas and Hercules. We are the Fool of the Tarot, the universal symbol of awakening. We all have the potential to step out into the world, however naïvely, believing our imagination is greater than convention.

Thank the gods for the entrepreneur; thank myth for the map of the journey. This is the story of how I started a business. Maybe it will inspire you to start your own.

{ I }

A Crisis of Meaning

Which is dearer, fame or your life? Which is greater, your life or possessions? Which is more painful, gain or loss?

LAO-TZU, *TAO TE CHING*

THE EYES that looked back at me from the mirror said it all: cold and cunning.

I was thirty-five years old, a vice-president of a major international public relations firm jetting around the world on an expense account. I had teams of people working for me in a dozen countries. I could be charming or ruthless, depending on what was demanded of me. The man I emulated, a few years my senior, was running the company's European operations. He had become one of the most powerful men in the PR business, climbing over his rivals by outworking and outsmarting them.

He was aggressive, seductive, and appealingly ugly, a fat Keith Richards without the drugs. He was also an unstoppable rainmaker for the firm.

I wanted to be powerful and successful too. I wanted the million-dollar bonus and the London brownstone, the expense account lifestyle that would allow me, on a whim, to fly to Paris for lunch, and the reputation as the firm's go-to guy. It would mean a long bloody climb, but I was willing to do almost anything to get it.

Perhaps it should have been a wake-up call when the man I so envied turned up dead in a London hotel room, murdered by a jealous husband. A Perrier bottle and a cheese knife were all it took to end a brilliant, if Machiavellian, career. His brutal, shocking death should have been a fire alarm shrieking at me to run for my life. It wasn't.

Instead, the wake-up call came silently, sneaking up on me one morning while I was shaving for work. It was as though something blurry came into sharp focus, slowly at first, then in high resolution. It's a strange feeling to look at your own eyes and suddenly see how hardened they have become. Serpent-like, they betrayed a willingness to strike to achieve a goal. They were the eyes of a corporate killer.

Where was the idealist who had wanted to write a really good novel, make a movie, and start a family? What happened to the guy who had sworn he would never allow money and ambition to displace his values? Like many people, I entered the workforce from university without much idea of what I could do to earn a living. I went into public relations because it seemed like the closest fit for my skills. I could string together a sentence, was a quick study, and had a sense of humor. I quickly learned to use these gifts to get what I thought I wanted.

Those ten years in the PR trenches changed me. The intense competition in a take-no-prisoners environment brought out the worst in me. I became someone who had no difficulty lobbying for the tobacco industry one day and pitching smoking cessation programs the next. I could make an industry that polluted half the world with its effluents look like a good corporate citizen, and I could do it without remorse. And in an office environment where politics and infighting were blood sports, I wasn't just surviving—I was thriving.

In my mind, what I did for a living wasn't a matter for moral judgment. I had convinced myself that in the business world there were trade-offs and compromises for everything. You couldn't have a vibrant economy if you weren't prepared to get an occasional bloody nose. That's why the world needed me, and my team of spin doctors: for when the industrial dreams had some downside risk. In the real world—where the real work of the economy occurred—things weren't black and white. They were . . . noir.

Those cold eyes in the shaving mirror told me what everyone who cared about me already knew: I was hopelessly lost. And when I looked harder, I saw that I was deeply unhappy. Funny how mundane a life-changing moment can be: shaving for work. One minute, you're looking at an ingrown hair; the next, you're looking at a character from Mad Men.

That was the moment that shifted everything. I suddenly felt exposed, like a vampire caught in the early morning sunlight. The man I was looking at was exactly what I swore to my college friends I would never become: the stereotypical business shark. It was a disturbing epiphany, but it launched a search for a missing person, the person I used to be. That was over thirty years ago.

THE DIRECTION HOME

What I saw in the mirror that morning caused me to take a long hard look at the direction of my life and especially at the compass I was using to set the course. In one of life's ironic twists, my reflection literally demanded reflection. Seeing

myself clearly for the first time in years ignited an inner conflict. I began to question everything that I had accepted about
what happiness and success really meant. That epiphany was
the genesis of this book.

This is a map of the territory that I discovered when I turned
my focus away from socially prescribed notions of "success"
and toward a place within myself, a place where real meaning
was possible. I've learned that meaning is primarily the work of
the heart, not the ego. Dr. Rachel Naomi Remen, the medical
pioneer and best-selling author, said it best: "The heart is an
organ of vision."[1] The heart teaches us to see that our lives are
a great gift when used in service to our deepest values, our loved
ones, and work that makes a difference in the world. In doing
so, it provides an alternate way of navigating the world around
us and, more importantly, of being in it.

Through the vision of the heart, I discovered that what I
knew about creating a meaningful life was ass-backward. I had
been chasing success in the misguided belief that it would make
me happy. Ironically, the more success I gained, the less happy
I became. I was an addict, needing more and more success to
overcome the growing sense of emptiness that I felt.

Like many of us, I was searching for meaning outside myself,
in the questionable values and ideals, and the illusions that I
had helped perpetuate through my work in PR. Edward Bernays,
the nephew of Sigmund Freud and father of the PR industry,
suggested as much when he speculated, "If we understand the
mechanism and motives of the group mind, is it now possible
to control and regiment the masses according to our will without their knowing about it?"[2]

Attempting to control and regiment the masses was a means
to an end for me. What I really wanted was to win, to make it
big. I failed to see that while I was busy manufacturing public demand, I was not immune to its indoctrination. The more
I believed in the cultural stereotype of "success," the easier it

was to pitch, and the more I pitched it, the more I believed it. That's where I got lost—in the combination of ambition, ruthless competition, and spin. Would it have happened if I had chosen accounting or engineering as my profession? Probably. My "fall" just happened a lot faster because the PR environment of the 1980s was a breeding ground for such falls.

People like me have made the single-minded pursuit of money, sex, and power in our culture normal and desirable. The unexamined lust for the American Dream, however, has fueled record-level consumer spending, unmanageable debt loads, and personal bankruptcy. I learned firsthand that the hidden price we pay for the pursuit of this Faustian nightmare is a gradual disconnection from whom and what we most love— our personal dreams, important relationships, and ultimately, our humanity. I saw too that to make my way out of the darkness that had swallowed me, I would need to replace ruthless ambition, unhealthy competition, and addiction to power with healthier values. Those drives had blinded me to what was most important, most meaningful. Ultimately, I would have to discover a new vision of success, one that didn't require me to sacrifice my humanity, happiness, values, or relationships in order to make a living and do well.

The discovery of my heart's vision was not instantaneous. It required many years of reflection and dedicated work to find and follow what had heart and meaning in my life. By reconnecting with that vision, I was eventually able to regain a sense of what most nourished my spirit and filled me with joy. I saw that my loved ones lived in my heart. My highest calling, my destiny, lived there too. The heart revealed what my mind could not: the truths of living and dying, the importance of love and companionship, how to care for family and friends, how to create meaningful work, and the love of community and the world. Ultimately, by reconnecting to the heart, I saw how to be human.

A PERSONAL DESTINY

You have a singular vision for your life, relationships, work, and community. You may not see it yet, but it waits patiently for you. It is not in your mind but in your own heart. Its secrets are available to you through commitment and practice.

Traveling the path of the heart, however, demands something of us, challenges us to grow into our best selves. The path of the heart asks us to trust; to use our gifts and talents to serve the heart, not the ego; and to build character on the journey. It asks that we turn down the volume on the self-critic and turn away from fears of not being enough or doing it right. Ultimately, it asks us to change.

Humans have always known about the visionary properties of the heart. The stories, legends, and myths of the world all give the same advice about direction and meaning: "Follow your heart." But how do we accomplish that in the cacophony of a marketplace culture spinning out of control? Angeles Arrien provides us with an ancient compass, one that I used to reenvision my life. She calls it the "four-chambered heart." The four-chambered heart is full, strong, open, and clear.[3]

Of course, the heart only delivers its vision when we engage it with reflection, insight, foresight, and purposeful action. Later in the book, I will explain these practices further, and finally, I will give you a personal action plan that comes from your own heart's vision, a plan that will carry you toward your own personal destiny.

I want to share with you what I learned the hard way. I believe this knowledge can help you address the questions you have about the direction of your life amid the turbulence of our times.

{ 2 }

A Great Darkness

Then the big Fish did swallow him, and he had done acts worthy of blame. Had it not been that he (repented and) glorified Allah, He would certainly have remained inside the Fish till the Day of Resurrection.

QUR'AN (37:142–44)

AN IDENTITY crisis, like the one I experienced, is only one of the ways the world can shake us awake. More often the awakening stems from a sudden (often difficult) change in circumstances: we lose a job, our marriage breaks up, we get cancer, our retirement savings disappear in the stock market, a loved one dies. The life that we know ends abruptly.

Change, particularly turbulent change, impacts our outer and inner lives. These sorts of radical disruptions demand that we take stock of what is most important. Suddenly we recognize that superficial values—how much money we earn, what car we drive, or what club we belong to—are far less important than we thought or were led to believe. Ask anyone who has faced serious calamity what is most important to them and usually they will give you the same answer: their lives, their families, and their friends. Almost everything else can be replaced.

But often we fail to act, even when we recognize the need to change course. We may continue to smoke or drink too much despite knowing full well that the odds favor an early visit to the mortician. Or we may walk on eggshells in a family relationship rather than talk about our concerns. Or we stay in a job that we hate because of procrastination or fear. In the moment, the short-term benefits of expediency, denial, and avoidance trump the long-term consequences. Many of us feel powerless to make the changes we know to be in our best interest.

I took the easy route as well. I had a life-changing epiphany while shaving for work one morning. I had recognized that I wasn't who I wanted to be, who I was meant to be. The truth about my ruthless drive for success was staring me in the face, and my response? I ignored it. I jumped right back into my high-velocity schedule.

I'd been shaken by what I'd seen in the mirror, but I had things to do and commitments to keep. I had innumerable reasons and excuses to not acknowledge what had happened. It was easier to drop back into my old habits and do exactly the same thing that created the dilemma in the first place than it was to change.

Unfortunately, that pattern of behavior is one of the most common causes of human suffering and sadness. Instead of deciding what I needed to change about my personal and professional life and making a plan to do it, I reassumed my old persona in the firm, allowing the mirror incident to fade like a bad dream. Instead of attempting to make changes, I threw myself into preparations for an intensive European media relations campaign to promote one of my most important client's products. Instead of taking time off to reenvision my life, I boarded a plane bound for Lausanne, Switzerland, the first of many stops over the next month. Luckily for me, this habitual pattern, so hard to interrupt, was about to create a perfect storm so powerful that I was forced to confront what I was racing to avoid. I was about to sink my own ship.

HITS

What matters most on a PR media tour is "hits." A hit is an article, feature story, column mention, radio or television interview, or other item of media attention you land for your client. It's the quid pro quo of the business. It's not lost on me today that I used to earn my living as a hit man.

Hits were the coin of the realm, and I was soon to discover that my European media tour was bankrupt. The people in our European offices who had helped me organize the tour decided not to tell me that they were having difficulties generating media interest. Most likely, they were afraid to suffer the consequences of not delivering. With a mere glance, I could send a junior account executive to the burn unit, a skill that was quickly proving its ineffectiveness. Intimidation, I was learning, did not motivate people to make the extra effort. Nor did it promote transparency.

The lack of hits became abundantly clear as the tour progressed. My clients and I went to a succession of press conferences in various countries to which nobody showed up . . . not one single journalist. Oh, maybe a friend of the account executive pretending to be a photojournalist would be on hand, snapping away with a camera, but no one with real press credentials. It was an unmitigated disaster. My clients were not amused. In fact, they were furious. They were paying me big bucks and getting no results, no interest, no hits. A sense of doom grew with every failed event.

The horror lasted for three grueling weeks. Finally, I landed in Paris, exhausted from the combination of travel, problem solving, fence mending with the client, temper tantrums from my colleagues, late-night phone calls to advance the tour, and panic attacks. I did not notice the Arc de Triomphe or the Eiffel Tower. Nor did I care to shop the Champs-Élysées. Paris might as well have been Cleveland. All I wanted to do was crawl into a quiet corner and disappear.

Emotionally and physically exhausted, I staggered to my room in the hotel and collapsed. For days I lay in bed, unable to sleep, unable to eat, unable to walk. All I could do was toss and turn like a man fallen overboard in a shipwreck, floating with the debris. A great darkness consumed me, a darkness that I could no longer outrun. I was haunted by questions that rolled over me like waves on a sandbar, eroding my best defenses. *What are you chasing? Money, status, and power? Why are you so addicted to success? Is it really worth the price? Look at you! You're a wreck. Why did you fail to heed the warning in the mirror? What's wrong with you, you asshole?*

I could no longer avoid the truth. My identity crisis returned, and this time it consumed me. I was finally, truly, utterly lost. The star that had guided my choices had burned out. My pursuit of success at any cost revealed the flaws in my philosophy and my character. Perhaps I was the last person to see them.

A ROLE MODEL FOR DARK TIMES

Although I didn't recognize it at the time, I wasn't the first person to be swallowed by the dark for failing to do the right thing. In fact, it's a common human trope recognized by numerous cultures throughout time. The story of falling into darkness comes from multiple traditions, including Greek, Etruscan,

Jewish, Muslim, and Haida. The story tells of the plight of one who becomes lost, only to find a new life on emerging from the darkness. In the Western tradition it is most commonly told as the story of Jonah and the whale. There are numerous versions of this story, including in the Qur'an and the Bible. Here is a version from the Old Testament.

When the Old Testament prophet Jonah was directed by God to preach repentance to his enemies, the Assyrians of Nineveh, he refused out of fear. Not only did he refuse, he took the first boat he could find headed in the opposite direction. At the time, Nineveh was corrupt, and the people there were pretty bad, sort of like Caracas, Venezuela, but way worse.

Jonah hopped a boat bound for Tarshish, seemingly oblivious to the fact that he was not invisible and that God was not only omniscient but also prone to anger. Perhaps because he was merely a minor prophet, Jonah also failed to foresee that God would be upset by his disobedience. God, of course, was not amused, and so he did what only gods can do: he sent a storm.

Jonah's shipmates were a shrewd bunch, though a little weak-hearted. They figured out pretty fast that they would be collateral damage in the wake of God's wrath, so they drew lots to determine who would toss Jonah overboard. Nobody knows which crewman drew the assignment to throw poor Jonah into the Mediterranean, but the job got done, and the storm stopped.

If drowning in the middle of the sea wasn't punishment enough, Jonah was promptly swallowed by a whale. God's not known for cutting corners. It is said that Jonah spent three days and nights in the whale's belly and, unlike Geppetto, who packed a candle, was in total darkness. There, Jonah asked for salvation. On the third day, Jonah was the beneficiary of the whale's indigestion (and God's parole plan) and was vomited onto shore. He was a mess but got with the program and made his way to Nineveh.

Since he was obviously good at setting limits and boundaries with consequences, God directed Jonah to deliver a warning of impending destruction. The city of Nineveh was given forty days to turn things around. The Assyrians were unexpectedly receptive. They took Jonah's warning seriously, perhaps because Jonah showed some signs of suffering consequences himself. His hair and skin had been bleached the color of bone by the whale's gastric acids, though his aroma may have been warning enough. The Assyrians donned sackcloth and ashes in repentance, and God spared Nineveh.

THE DARK NIGHT OF THE SOUL

The whale is the animal totem of those thrown into the deep by inner or outer turbulence. Whales symbolize the energies of death and rebirth, a mythic cycle that each person, committed to being their best self, must undergo to gain the personal liberation necessary to change.

Like Jonah, when we are driven by fear or confusion, we are unable to make wise choices that support our own best selves. Often, it takes an act of God, fate, or circumstance (depending on your worldview) to plunge us deeply enough in the waters of the heart for liberation to occur. There, we are swallowed by a personal darkness that we cannot escape without rigorous self-examination and a change of heart. In the darkness, we must examine the premises we built our lives on, review the choices we made, and confront the truth. Ultimately, we must ask ourselves a question that can only be answered in the belly of the whale, where we are utterly alone. What gives life meaning?

We must all confront this question at various times in our lives. Major life transitions—work, relationships, health, finances, and aging—provoke a deeper look at what makes life meaningful. As well, the experience of loss, disillusionment, or suffering can be so powerfully motivating that we can no longer abide the pain of stasis.

The myths and stories of the world are filled with tales where the hero or heroine is swallowed by the unknown. Osiris, Hercules, Finn MacCool, and Red Riding Hood are all examples of this recurring theme. Another famous example of the transformational power of the dark night of the soul comes from the story of Paul, the apostle of Jesus, who was blinded by a flash of light on the road to Damascus. Like Jonah, Paul was cast into darkness for three days until he recognized the error of his ways and changed course from persecuting Christians to leading them. His question, "What would you have me do?" is the primal koan for every person who has been consumed by the whale, whether asked of a personal deity, or of their best self.

C. S. Lewis, popularly known as the author of the Narnia children's books, experienced his own dark night upon the death of his beloved wife, Joy Davidman. Writing under the pseudonym N. W. Clerk, Lewis chronicled his inner journey from grief to acceptance in his book A Grief Observed. He entered the darkness through loss, a particularly difficult underworld journey that all of us must make at some time in our lives. "Nothing less will shake a man—or at any rate a man like me—out of his merely verbal thinking and his merely notional beliefs," he writes. "He has to be knocked silly before he comes to his senses. Only torture will bring out the truth. Only under torture does he discover it himself."[1]

Nelson Mandela is a modern Jonah. For twenty-seven years, Mandela was imprisoned for his fight to end apartheid in South Africa. By his own admission, he entered prison as an angry man who favored armed resistance as head of the military wing of the African National Congress. He left his prison cell as a man of peace. In a letter to his then wife, Winnie, Mandela wrote: "The cell is an ideal place to learn to know yourself . . . Honesty, sincerity, simplicity, humility, purity, generosity, absence of vanity, readiness to serve your fellow men [are] qualities within the reach of every soul."[2]

Mandela proposes an optimist's view of being whale bait, a view that is apparently shared by psychiatrist Gerald D. May. Dr. May suggests that the dark night of the soul is a form of benign transformation. While the darkness may hold terrors, they are largely the ego's entitled protests at its own loss of authority. He writes,

> The dark night is a profoundly good thing. It is an ongoing spiritual process in which we are liberated from attachments and compulsions and empowered to live and love more freely. Sometimes this letting go of old ways is painful, occasionally even devastating. But this is not why the night is called "dark." The darkness of the night implies nothing sinister, only that the liberation takes place in hidden ways, beneath our knowledge and understanding. It happens mysteriously, in secret, and beyond our conscious control. For that reason it can be disturbing or even scary, but in the end it always works to our benefit.[3]

I didn't think it was such good news to be having a miserable breakdown in the belly of that Paris hotel room. Unlike Jonah, I didn't pray for salvation while I was lying exhausted. Nor did I reflect on religious conversion, the nature of personal freedom, ending war, solving hunger, or becoming a saint. Quite frankly, I was too tired to come up with either an idea or a strategy that would require me to move. All I could do was surrender to the dark.

I had been finally and completely undone by the worship of the small god of success. That undoing, though, was precisely the preparation I needed to learn my lesson.

{ 3 }

The Jonah Lessons

You can't keep a good man down.

PROVERB

THE STORY of Jonah teaches us—those who have been plunged into the darkness—that there is work to do. It does no good to rage at our plight, make bargains, or plead for mercy—all stages before acceptance. The darkness cannot be dispelled by emotional outbursts. We must accept that we have been overtaken. We can complain, rail, and gnash our teeth, but it gets us no closer to locating the light switch.

The Jonah story teaches us that darkness is not a place where we are sent for punishment. Had that been God's intention for Jonah, drowning would have provided capital punishment in spades. Instead, Jonah is swallowed for purgation, a process that demands reflection, surrender, and a change of heart. An omnipotent force swallows us, placing us in a mythic cycle of death and rebirth, where we are called to face who and what we are. Only when we understand our true calling, when we've connected to a higher vision for our lives, can we be reborn.

Soul searching is the hard labor of every Jonah. First, we must purge ourselves of the illusions, fears, and false values that have led to our arrest. Then we must examine the past, recognize our errors, and repent. From this we are able to gain enough clarity to return to the world with a renewed sense of purpose and direction. Our release from darkness comes only when we commit to doing what matters most. Even in mythology, a spontaneous enlightenment seldom occurs. We are in the best company with Siddhartha, the enlightened Buddha, who had to put in serious time and effort under the Bodhi tree before he attained his transformation.

The teachings of darkness can take many years to harvest, and gathering them is hard work. It certainly was for me. There are five key lessons that I learned from reflecting on my own dark night of the soul and from the story of Jonah and the whale:

1. STOP

When we ignore the warning signs (as I had) and are plunged into darkness, we must stop doing whatever it was that led to the crisis in the first place. Many of us are so invested in a point of view, a course of action, or a pattern of behavior that we cannot stop because it is all we know. I bypassed the first opportunity to change by throwing myself into work and speeding past it. Like Jonah, my escape attempt was driven by fear of the unknown and the familiarity of habitual behavior. Sometimes, doing the wrong thing seems like the easier path. The very habits that had led me astray also insulated me from asking the hard questions.

Change can seem difficult and scary. For me, confronting the future without the structure of the past—even when that structure is a rickety scaffold doomed to collapse—required a faith I could not summon. Instead, I chose to ignore the warning signs of unhappiness and bully my way across Europe. In a metaphorical sense, I was thrown overboard by my colleagues. Eventually, I succumbed to exhaustion in Paris.

When darkness overcomes us, attempting to move in any direction is reckless. Stripped of our ability to see a way forward— or a way out—we are gripped by a transformative process that we do not command. All we can do in the belly of the whale is give up any notion of control, let go of our agenda, and surrender. That surrender can take three days, three weeks, or three years. It is up to us. Fear or stubbornness dictates the length of our stay.

Once we surrender, we learn to access stillness. Stillness is the place within us, beyond the ego's reach, that can only be found once we let go of stress, anxiety, anger, resentment, ambition, and other drivers that keep us locked into a particular pattern and disconnected from our own inner guidance. "Within you there is a stillness and a sanctuary," wrote Hermann Hesse, "to which you can retreat at any time and be yourself."[1]

Stillness was not easy for me to find. My mind was constantly churning, planning, and scheming. But learning to quiet the mind is one of the most important apprenticeships of the dark. It takes commitment and a set of practices that we will explore later in the book. And it takes the fruit of a long stretch in darkness—patience.

Ultimately, stillness provides us sanctuary, and once we have entered it, we know that we can return there anytime, that we can come home to ourselves. With dedicated work, we see what is most heartfelt and meaningful, what is most important to our lives.

2. MANAGE YOUR FEARS

Jonah was scared, and fear led him to make bad decisions. His fears were undermining his best interests—represented here by the God of the Old Testament—and those fears were carrying him in the opposite direction of his highest purpose. The lesson here is that we must never make life choices when we are afraid. When we allow our fears to overcome us, we are carried off course. Like Jonah on the boat to Tarshish, we are unable to discern what is in our own best interest, the interests of the people we care about, and the interest of our mission in the world.

Fear never helps us when we are in the dark. It only promotes greater terrors by seizing our imagination and turning it against us, demonizing the future. As long as we allow fear to control us, the work of surrender, reflection, and discernment cannot be accomplished. Our energy is diverted to feeding fear instead of searching our hearts for guidance.

Neither the past nor the future hold the power to quell our fears. The only place we can find solace is here and now. Learning to stay in the present moment helps us meet reality as it unfolds, rather than succumb to terrors of what might befall us.

3. TRUST

The remedy for fear is trust. Jonah mistrusted God, mistrusted the Assyrian reception of God's word, and mistrusted his ability to carry out God's orders. Because he didn't believe he could accomplish God's task, he ran away.

I too was on the run. I hopped on a plane to Europe rather than trust that I could find the answers that would lead me to the better self that I had abandoned for misguided notions of "success." My failure to trust what I knew in my heart to be true accelerated an inner conflict, and I faced that conflict only after I had exhausted myself enough to stop running.

This, of course, is a central lesson of the Jonah story. In myth, the inner conflict is extroverted. While it is unlikely that a large fish will swallow us, the possibility that we will be cast into darkness by our own actions if we do not listen to inner guidance is far more realistic. We are imprisoned there so that we have a chance to change course. This "sea change" requires that we replace fear with trust. We are asked to trust that, even though our situation may be difficult, we have what it takes to find clarity. We must also trust that we have the inner resources to carry out our mission and find a pathway to greater happiness and peace of mind. Trust delivers us from self-abandonment, the destination that our fear would set for us. Through trust, we begin to see a direction home to what has heart and meaning in our lives. Even when we can't see this clearly, we must trust that we have the capacity to find the inner compass.

4. LISTEN

There is no record of what Jonah did while he was captive in the whale's belly, though he did repent. We can speculate that he was in shock at discovering himself in solitary confinement and that he felt frightened, overwhelmed, and alone.

Those who have experienced the dark night of the soul can undoubtedly empathize with Jonah's plight. They recognize the horror of entombment in the past, in old ways of thinking and being. They understand the futility of breathing new life into a fallen identity. Also, they know that trying to resuscitate the drowned corpse of the past is futile.

The belly of the whale is a paradox. It is the one place where the price of liberty is complete surrender. When we cannot figure things out or see a way forward, we are forced to surrender to guidance from a source other than the ego or our old bad habits. This requires us to listen. But listen to what?

In the Old Testament, Jonah was required to listen to God's direction and take action on the promises made. We too have a covenant to keep. Beneath the chatter of our fears and the mistaken agenda of the ego is another voice. This is the wisdom voice of the heart. It is always available to us, providing guidance in accordance with our highest values. In stillness and through reflection, its messages can be heard, directing us toward what's most important to our lives—whom and what we love, what work is worth doing, and how to be happy no matter what our circumstances might be. We must act on these instructions.

Of course, the refusal to obey a power greater than his own fear was Jonah's undoing. The calamity that befell him as a result is a reminder that there are always consequences of our choices. In his book *The Power of Myth*, Joseph Campbell suggests that Jonah's mistake is a common one: "The world is full of people who have stopped listening to themselves or have listened only to their neighbors to learn what they ought to do, how they ought to behave, and what the values are they should be living for."[2]

That would have described me thirty years ago. I had been caught up in the pursuit of "success," driven by values that led me further and further away from myself. Those values led me to a state of exhaustion and burnout, to a profound unhappiness. Arrested by the darkness in my hotel room in Paris, I was no longer capable of chasing what I thought I wanted. I was forced to confront the false values that I had accepted so easily as the currency of success. I wished then that I had stayed connected to my heart and listened to its directions. Instead, I allowed that guidance to be drowned out by the cacophony of my own ambition and the allure of a high-consumption lifestyle that I thought was the chief measure of a meaningful life.

5. MAKE CHANGES

Ultimately, the lesson of Jonah is about change. Those who have been plunged into darkness through their allegiance to personal gain, or by a turbulent world, have a choice. We can remain in the belly of the whale, held there by the confusions of the ego, or we can choose to align ourselves with the wisdom of the heart.

With that choice a fundamental transformation comes about. We are no longer solely governed by the material values of the world around us. We are no longer subject to the willful struggle to uphold the ego's agenda. We begin to hear the soft sounds of the heart and begin to understand that there is a deeper guidance available to each of us. The more we attend to the voice of the heart, the stronger its direction becomes.

That surrender accomplished, our salvation begins. We are deposited, like Jonah, on a new shore. There, what we must be and what we must do begin to form. Freed from the turbulence of the mind and the world, we gain the ability to start to reenvision life.

ARRESTED FOR TRANSFORMATION

After days of lying immobile counting the ceiling tiles from my hotel bed, my will to live began to return slowly. I managed to bathe, feed, and clothe myself. Eventually, I was able to leave the dark hotel room and venture out onto the dark streets of Montmartre, a neighborhood in the north of Paris. I was not yet a new man. In fact, I was more like a wobbly ghost. While Jonah had been bleached white by gastric acids, I had been rendered almost transparent by exhaustion.

Walking the cobbled streets, I thought, would allow me to collect my scattered thoughts and feelings. They were still washing up like debris on the beach. I passed the bars and bistros, the boulangeries and fromageries. I passed sex shops and peep

shows. I passed the windmill of the Moulin Rouge. I wasn't looking closely at any of it. Since the whale had disgorged me, my
gaze was turned inward, focused on the wreck of my former life.

Walking, I told myself, was exactly the medicine I needed to
put myself back together. So I walked and walked and walked. I
thought about my former boss and mentor meeting his end in
a hotel room in London. My demise in the hotel room in Paris
was not quite as final. I had lost an identity but not my life. This
international PR assignment was a rocket, my boss had told me
when I was first assigned to the account a couple of years earlier: my career was going to take off to new heights. That rocket
had fallen from the heavens and crash-landed in Montmartre.

I was surprised by how little I cared about any of that now.
I felt oddly detached, as though the past three weeks were a
dim memory of a fever dream. I didn't care anymore about hits.
I didn't care about winning. I didn't care about "making it."
What I cared about, as I walked the streets, was my family. I
missed home, my wife, and my daughter. I missed our house,
our bed, and the smell of coffee in the morning. I missed walking in the park across the street and watching the children play
at the playground.

I cared about putting myself back together, but I didn't know
how to accomplish it. My life was a puzzle, and there were
pieces broken and missing: things that no longer fit together.
The model for living that I had been busy building had been lost
in an ocean of ambition. Raising the wreckage didn't seem like
the thing to do. What I needed was a new model. At the time, I
had absolutely no idea what it would look like. What I was sure
of, though, was that I would need to take a long hard look into
my heart to uncover it. And I would need to act.

{ 4 }

What Matters Most

Your work is to discover your work

And then with all your heart

To give yourself to it.

UNKNOWN

S OMEHOW, I recovered enough strength to board a
plane home. The European media tour had been a
disaster. I had hit rock bottom, probably the only
thing powerful enough to shake me awake and force me to look
at making some important changes to my life. I took solace in
the knowledge that in a few hours I would be back with my wife
and daughter; I would be home.

When I left on the tour, my daughter, Alannah, was just three
weeks old. It had been very hard to leave, but I felt duty bound.

Now, at almost eight weeks, I wondered how she had changed, what she would look like, who she would be. Having been adopted as a toddler, I had never had the experience of knowing blood kin. Most people take their biological families for granted; orphans do not. I had wanted to experience a genetic bond more than anything in the world. My baby daughter was a dream come true. Thinking about my wife and newborn daughter was the only thing that had gotten me through the shipwreck in Paris. My life with them was the one thing I was still certain about. I couldn't wait to get home.

I landed at Toronto Pearson airport, struggled into a cab, and directed the driver to our large apartment overlooking High Park in the leafy west end of the city. I paid the cabbie and climbed up the long stairway to the house. It was like a waking dream. My arms and legs were so heavy I could barely climb from one step to the next. I was tired from the long crummy flight in the back of the plane, and I had a hangover from too much free booze. I felt like Rip van Winkle, away not for just three weeks but for years. Everything looked familiar but somehow different—smaller, older, more weather-beaten than I remembered. Maybe I was just seeing myself reflected in the surroundings.

Finally, I made it to the porch and opened our heavy front door. Unfortunately, the reception was not how I imagined it would be, not the reunion I'd hoped for. My wife, Lynne, looked relieved to see me, but I could tell instantly that she was angry. I hugged her, but the hug back was reserved, cool. The formalities finished, she pulled away abruptly.

I took in my surroundings. Lynne had obviously made an extra effort to get the house ready for my return: there were fresh flowers and the smell of baking, and the house was impeccably clean. But my beautiful wife looked haggard, as if she had been up all night. It all began to come into horrible focus: I had left her to care for a newborn baby with no support, and she was upset. I had left the family at a critical time, too wrapped up in my own ambitions to think about the impact an extended business trip would have on the family. Our child was not a sound sleeper, and Lynne was exhausted from having to pull double duty while I was away.

I was just doing my job, I protested to myself, employing the accomplice's alibi. Until that point, I had never questioned leaving for an extended business trip. I accepted work as the top priority no matter what was happening at home. It was business, after all. That rationale, so logical before my daughter's birth, now sounded like the weakest argument imaginable. Why hadn't I foreseen that leaving would cause my wife such exhaustion and stress?

If Lynne was frosty at the reunion, the baby was terrified. Every time I tried to hold her, she screamed herself purple, as though I was a stranger! Of course I was a stranger. Technically speaking, I had been away over half of her life. Dutiful father that I thought I was, I'd brought her the cutest outfit: tiny overalls, a golden sweater, and a matching T-shirt from an exclusive children's shop in Paris. The gifts seemed of little import now. My daughter's screams shattered any remaining fantasy I held of returning to the warm embrace of family.

THE SHORTSIGHTED WISH

The story of King Midas, a classical myth, depicts this dynamic but with far more tragic consequences. Midas, an adopted son himself, finds the satyr Silenus passed out drunk in his rose garden. Silenus is the beloved tutor of the god Dionysus. In return for taking care of the sodden Silenus, Dionysus grants Midas a wish. Midas wishes that everything he touches should turn to gold.

In haste, and with a growing lust for wealth and power, Midas begins touching things—his roses, tree branches, household objects—and amasses a golden fortune.

Inadvertently, he gets around to the family. With a slight brush of the hand, Midas accidentally turns his beloved daughter to gold. There are two endings to this story. In one version, King Midas is unable to feed himself and starves to death because of his shortsighted wish. In another, Dionysus takes pity on the grief-stricken king. Midas is instructed to cleanse himself in the river Pactolus, releasing the golden touch to the waters.

This is a timeless reminder to those of us who believe that the riches of the world hold a solution to all our problems. The story of Midas is reenacted on a daily basis, whether we pursue success with the single-mindedness of a young executive, or like a titan who fails to recognize the dire consequences of their all-consuming addiction to power.

The god of intoxication—here represented by Dionysus—fills us with a blinding need to satisfy empty places within ourselves by acquiring things. The satyr is a metaphor for an out-of-control consumer society—drunk, unconscious, and driven by base needs. We disconnect from the natural beauty within us, symbolized here by the rose garden, and lose ourselves in the shortsighted acquisition of golden objects. We regain our senses only when we discover, in horror, that what we really need has been mortally sacrificed for what we think we need. At this point, we have a choice. We can remain addicted and end up famished for what we have lost, or we can immerse ourselves in the river of the heart, which cleanses and releases us from a wish that has become a curse.

COMING HOME

Eventually, my baby daughter stopped screaming when I held her, and my wife forgave me for being away. I realized, in retrospect,

that I had presented Lynne with no choice about the trip. It was
a fait accompli. In fact, I felt I had no choice about going. It was
my job. I felt swept up by a current that I could not resist and
obligations that I could not change. Clearly, I had a lot of thinking to do about my life. Here were three wake-up calls in a row:
the mirror, the darkness in Paris, and finally, a child who didn't
know me. I could no longer ignore the signs. I was not taking
care of business. I was not taking care of my family. And I was
not taking care of myself.

I was deeply shaken. When we leave something of value
behind—and know it—we feel a sense of dislocation. We recognize that life has not been static in the interim. Indeed, like
a growing child, life has progressed independently without
ever needing us to advance its narrative. I had met many people over the years—men and women—who carried scars from
their inability to be present for the people they most loved.
Whether they were consumed by their work, caught up in the
pursuit of material wealth, or preoccupied by worry or doubt,
their absence cost them something dear. They got quiet when
they talked about it, wistful over what they sacrificed for other
obligations. In retrospect, they assured me, whatever they were
chasing, or chained to, was worth far less than the price. I did
not wish to remain in their company.

What matters most? I wondered. I needed to locate myself in
that question and take an inventory of what I found there. I went
for long walks in the park across from our flat and had deep
conversations with my wife as I struggled to figure out how to
correct the course of my life. I knew that to ask myself these
questions from a place of anguish and self-reproach would
result in a set of answers that were predictably maudlin and
mundane. The focus would be on what hadn't worked and what
was wrong with me, and on the past rather than the present.
While I couldn't deny that my approach to life had some serious
flaws, there were also things that worked well and had merit. It

would have been easy to forget that and severely limit my ability to reenvision my life by looking only at the mistakes.

However, I could not pretend that I was happy. Of all the recent wake-up calls, my child's terror at my touch was clearly the most painful. I did not want a golden touch at the cost of starving to death emotionally. I had seen the effects of isolation on some people at work. Rather than address their pain, they threw themselves, like the satyr Silenus, deeper into work, alcohol, and drug abuse. But hidden beneath a thin, golden veneer of independence, competency, and success, the loneliness remained. The more they worked, the less companionable they became. Something brittle took over, perhaps a sense of resigned acceptance of the lonely monastery of their desks at work.

When I looked deeper at my own condition, I began to see that business per se was not the problem. It was my approach to business that I needed to review and change. Something was driving me to pursue success with a single-minded ruthlessness that scared everyone around me. Now that I could see it, it scared me too. I would need to fill that empty place in myself with something other than a Midas touch or risk turning my family relationships to stone. After Paris, that was a sacrifice I was no longer prepared to make.

Strangely, what I did for a living—public relations—no longer held the same grip on my imagination that it had before the media tour. I no longer wanted to make my living hyping products. That had died in the belly of the whale. But what else could I do? I needed to take care of my family. I couldn't just walk away from a career. I wanted to create something of value through my work, but I had no immediate answer to what to do next. Nor would I for quite some time.

And although the shock of my painful homecoming underscored the importance of my family, I could see that family was not the remedy either. I loved my wife and baby daughter. That commitment was made even more obvious by seeing the effect of being away at a time when my presence was not only required, it was critical. But the idea of trading obsessions—work for family—didn't strike me as a particularly healthy exchange. What I needed was to find a both/and solution, not an either/or solution. Ultimately, what I really needed to do was to reconnect to the river of my own heart and cleanse myself in it.

{ 5 }

The Labyrinth

How beautiful the world would be if there were

a procedure for moving through labyrinths.

UMBERTO ECO

L EAVING THE security of what you already know—what
you've mastered—for the unknown can be challenging work. At least that's how I felt as I began to
grapple with figuring out how to change my own life. There
were two things that were made immediately clear to me.

The first was what I didn't want. I could no longer tolerate the cutthroat environment of a large international public
relations firm, even though I had learned to dominate it. I recognized that my own ruthlessness was reinforced and fueled by
the ruthlessness around me. But thinking about what to do next

led only to blind alleys and dead ends. I could not see anything to do that wouldn't leave me in the same conundrum. I didn't think that business was intrinsically bad. Work could be ennobling when conducted with values and principles. What was bad was how I was working.

The second thing that was clear to me was what I wanted to keep: my family. Being with my wife and daughter, and having our family grow closer, was now of paramount importance to me. My daughter's screams at my homecoming made that fact abundantly clear. It was a wake-up call that I would not forget.

Beyond that, I didn't really know what I wanted and needed to be happy. The lust for power and success had driven me into a kind of labyrinth, one that led me further and further away from myself, and away from the people whom I most loved. I got there using a bad compass to set my course, fashioned from the cardinal illusions that I had helped manufacture through PR. By believing that a meaningful life is acquired in the marketplace, I had come to measure my personal worth by my net worth. That falsehood fueled the pursuit of material wealth and power. It was a way to prove my value to myself and then prove it to the world around me. That route—one that had been interrupted by a series of "fortunate setbacks"—was leading to moral bankruptcy. As luck would have it, I had gained an opportunity to retrace my steps and rethink my path.

THE MINOTAUR

Legend tells us that the Minotaur had the head of a bull and the body of a man. This unfortunate birth defect (but the desired transformation of every stock market trader) was the product of strange mating practices between the Minotaur's mom, Queen Pasiphae, and a white bull. The bull was apparently beautiful, but that alone did not entirely explain the queen's lust. She was the target of revenge by the god Poseidon.

Poseidon conjured the bull from the sea and gave it to Pasiphae's husband, King Minos, who asked for a sign that Cretans
were favored by the gods. Minos was then supposed to sacrifice
the bull to Poseidon. Minos refused to carry out the offering
because the white bull was magnificent, and he decided that
he wanted it for breeding purposes. Strangely, he got his wish.

Poseidon wreaked revenge on Minos like a mob boss. He
went after generations of the king's family, turning Pasiphae
into a zoophile and the offspring of her union with the bull
into a Minotaur. This appears to have been a reasonably pop-
ular consequence in the ancient world, where centaurs, satyrs,
manticores, and sphinxes apparently abounded, the hybrid offspring of questionable moral choices.

Minos decided to enlist a contractor, Daedalus, to build
the Labyrinth, a huge holding pen for his monstrous illegiti-
mate son. Each year, fourteen young people—seven boys and
seven girls—from neighboring Athens were led into the Labyrinth and fed to the Minotaur as tributes in the original Hunger
Games. Like the Hunger Games, this too was an act of revenge,
payback for the assassination of Minos's son, Androgeus, who
was in Athens at an athletic competition. When the Athenians
either refused to or could not identify the murderer, King Minos
decided that the penalty should be an annual tributes' dinner
with the Minotaur.

Enter Theseus, the hero. Theseus's superpower was wisdom
(a power that predictably deserted him in middle age). Theseus
decided to solve the problem of the Minotaur's tribute buffet by
volunteering to take the place of one of their number. He was
aided in his quest to kill the Minotaur by King Minos's daughter
Ariadne. Apparently, Ariadne shared her mother's predisposi-
tion to infatuation, falling in love with Theseus at first sight.
Ariadne consulted her father's contractor, Daedalus, about
the specs for the labyrinth. She was advised to go forward and
always down, never left or right.

Like a ninja, Theseus entered the labyrinth at night, with the directions, a concealed weapon, and a ball of golden thread. He tied the thread to the doorpost and began stalking his prey. According to legend, the Minotaur was dispatched with a slash to the throat, or was strangled, depending on the source. Theseus, following the thread, retraced his steps and escaped the crime scene with the girl.

FORWARD AND DOWN

Figuring out what's most important, especially when you've lost your way, can be like walking a labyrinth. Many of us get stuck making predictable turns to the left or the right to fit in socially or culturally. It's what we're expected to do, who we're expected to be. Like the Athenian tributes making their annual march to meet the hungry Minotaur, we find ourselves locked into a prescribed footpath made by those who walked before us, one that leads to a predictable destination. Many of us march stoically toward our rendezvous with the monster, fulfilling our obligations and never questioning the journey. We take our place in what Angeles Arrien terms "the procession of the living dead."

Others are like the hero, Theseus. They enter the maze as a matrix of transformation, a symbolic, initiatory passageway from one life to another. To find their way, they stop and wrestle with some tough questions: Where am I now? Who do I want to be? Where do I really want to go? How do I get there? Rather than accept a culturally prescribed and predictably mundane destiny, they choose to do the courageous work of finding their own way out of confusion. This is the journey of the self-made.

To make our way out of a labyrinth of the mind—for that is where the maze truly exists—we must first understand how it is constructed. The labyrinth is made from our fears and held together by repetitive choices. Our fears are twofold. The first fear is that the monster within us, imprisoned at the center of our psyche, might destroy us. This Minotaur, who we will meet in depth in the next chapter, is the inner voice of the imposter or the self-critic. Unmanaged and unbounded, it devours our best self and renders us lost.

The second fear is that we will never find our way out of the box. Logic cannot penetrate a paradox; linear thinking offers no guidance to an irrational and mercurial puzzle that threatens our very identity. We must therefore rely on other ways to tackle our problem of life purpose and direction. Don't despair. To vanquish these fears and solve the puzzle, we have two powerful allies: Ariadne and Daedalus.

Ariadne reminds us to stay connected to who and what we love. She is the mistress of the Labyrinth and provides us with the golden thread that leads us to and from the encounter with the monster. The golden thread, Ariadne's lifeline, is known in mythology as a *clew*, an archaic variant to our word *clue*.[1] It is the connector that we must hold on to as our old perspectives are rearranged. What threads our lives together are the people, places, activities, causes, and things that are deeply meaningful. These are all clues—landmarks—that lead us forward and that inform our preferred future.

Daedalus, the labyrinth builder, also provides us with valuable insight in this quest. He is a stand-in for ourselves as master problem solvers; it is his advice that we must heed if we are to find liberation. Go forward and always down.

Forward is not only a direction. It is also a time frame. When we cast our vision from the present into the future, we have an opportunity to leave the mistakes of the past behind us. Rather than obsessing over what went wrong and repeating old patterns, we must recognize that the present moment is a powerful leverage point for change. That doesn't mean that we forget the past; it just means that we don't repeat it. We learn from our trials and failures and apply those lessons to taking steps in a new direction.

Many of us become lost and disoriented by searching the outer landscape for clues and solutions to inner problems. "Always down" reminds us to look inward, to the heart for direction. The mind can become easily disoriented by complex and confusing life challenges. Transition points can be perplexing and dispiriting, causing us to doubt our ability to solve their puzzles. Daedalus suggests that taking a different direction than we would by habit solves the labyrinth.

Before we can follow the golden thread forward and always down, we must prepare ourselves for the journey. We cannot walk the labyrinth blindly, like some appetizer for the ravenous Minotaur. We must gather ourselves through careful preparation. As the authors of *The Book of Symbols* so elegantly suggest, the way to a new life requires us to navigate "confusion and clarity, multiplicity and unity, imprisonment and liberation, chaos and order."[2]

We must also prepare to meet the Minotaur . . . and defeat it.

{ 6 }

The Monster Within

Our deepest fears are like dragons guarding our deepest treasures.

RAINER MARIA RILKE

I MADE TWO important decisions to begin the journey out of my maze of faulty values. First, I needed to leave public relations. I could now see how Machiavellian I had become in the shark tank. I didn't want to end up like my old boss, whose values—or lack of them—got him killed. Second, I needed to search for the better self I'd lost chasing power and success.

Knowing I had to leave my job and actually leaving it were two different things. With bills to pay and a young family to care for, I couldn't just up and quit. What I could do immediately was make an oath to leave in a year's time. That would give me a solid twelve months to plan and prepare before making the leap.

A leap to where, I still didn't know—that's where the second priority kicked in.

The status quo, even when you hate it, is oddly seductive.

The one-year buffer was as sensible as it was dangerous. There was always the chance I could be sucked back into the PR vortex like a Kansas farmhouse in tornado season. While my epiphany had been powerful, I could feel its hold over me weakening a little every day. And while I'd committed to finding a new career, my work at the agency was actually becoming even more demanding. The economy had weakened, and our profit margins were eroding as clients reduced budgets. We were directed to identify which team members were expendable and prepare for layoffs. On top of all this, I had a new boss and he didn't seem to like me much, perhaps because I didn't like him either.

To move forward I needed a plan—a plan I didn't have. Worse, I didn't know how to make one that wasn't stuck in the past. Obviously, I would have to think and act differently; I would have to be driven less by my ambition and more by my heart and character. What I did know was that I wanted to do meaningful work, work that was guided by healthy values. I also wanted to be of service, to make a difference. These were the same aspirations I'd had when I graduated from university, before I had allowed them to languish.

SELF-HELP

Weeks of worry followed. No matter how hard I tried, I could not envision a new career path. The agency was even more tension filled. The threat of layoffs turned the office into a supercollider of accelerated nastiness.

The combination of knowing I was finished with the business and the fear that it might be finished with me first had me worried. A performance review with my new boss confirmed I was on the bubble. It wasn't so much what he said. It was what he had written across the top page of my review: "More problems inside than out." He either didn't notice or didn't care that I could read upside down.

He'd nailed it, though. I was in trouble with my coworkers in the Toronto office and abroad. Years of bullying to get what I wanted had made me a target. Of course, I'd seen it before. Senior management encouraged you to be ruthlessly aggressive, and then eventually fired you for it. An occasional shark sacrifice kept the rest of the fish swimming with just the right combination of tension and relief. It may have been the agency's only employee morale policy.

"More problems inside than out" was also a perfect description of the inner turmoil that consumed my thoughts. At work I pretended that everything was fine and dandy. Some words in existentialist philosopher Albert Camus's novel A Happy Death fit my state of mind at the time: as one character says, "I feel like getting married, or committing suicide, or subscribing to L'Illustration. Something desperate, you know."[1] When you've lost your way, "something desperate" can seem like the obvious choice, the inevitable choice. It was that growing sense of desperation that forced me into the world of self-help.

One morning, I read an article in a local business magazine about Martin Rutte, a management consultant and "self-help guru." Martin's program was about creating a new vision for your life, one that was focused on making a valuable contribution to society. It was called the Success Factor. The word "success" caught my eye. Of course: it had been my Achilles heel. I still wanted to be successful, but I needed to find a new, more balanced way to achieve it. The notion that success included making a meaningful contribution was an intriguing one. It sounded exactly like the combination I was looking for in a new career. I had never considered going to a self-help program, in fact, I would have been willing to bet against the possibility. Self-help, like PR, was a sideshow for hawkers and hucksters. I was too savvy to fall for their shtick. Or so I thought. Cynical but desperate, I held my nose and enrolled in the course.

When I arrived at a downtown hotel on a Saturday morning for the first day of the Success Factor seminar, I found twenty or so oddballs gathered there. They appeared to be a strange collection of losers, misfits, and insurance salesmen. One guy was a dead ringer for George Costanza from *Seinfeld*. Another, wearing sweats, looked like he had just come from the gym. Two women in pastel pantsuits were engaged in a high-pitched conversation punctuated by shrill laughter. The hotel, which had seen its best days in the sixties, was a lot shabbier than ones I frequented in New York and Paris. I made sure I took the seat closest to the exit.

Martin Rutte arrived ten minutes later. He was meticulously dressed in a business suit and tie, as congenial as he was self-assured. In explaining his premise, Martin proposed that maybe work can be both lucrative and fulfilling; that maybe it's not an either/or proposition. *Cult leader*, I thought to myself.

Fighting my urge to flee, I watched the proceedings from behind a mask of imperiousness, an affectation I had mastered from bullying junior account executives. In truth, I was afraid. I was clearly out of my element, filled with self-doubt, and way beyond my comfort zone. Martin stated that everyone in the room had a unique vision for their life, but it would take some digging to find it.

I considered his premise with defensive agitation. What if I didn't have a unique vision? What if his spiel was nonsense? I hadn't spent a lot of time navel gazing in my career; the time I had spent in reflection had been the result of setbacks. And how was this digging going to take place? I hoped I wouldn't be asked to do some touchy-feely new age stuff like staring into someone's eyes for an hour or going on a "trust walk." Not with this crowd.

There are two conversations in which we engage: the public dialogue that we have with others, and the private internal monologue that we have about everything that is happening around us. My internal monologue kicked into high gear when Martin asked us to introduce ourselves to another participant in the group and talk about what had drawn us to the workshop. I paired up with a pleasant-looking middle-aged woman, an administrative assistant to a financial planner. I barely listened to what she was saying. I wasn't trying to be rude; I was just too busy talking to myself about the blunder I had made in coming. *What on earth were you thinking? This is a freak show! You're talking to a stranger about how lost you are!*

Despite the conversation in my head, I did manage to hear something the woman said. Her plainspoken declaration managed to reach me through the internal roar of fears, doubts, cynicism, and confusion. "I know my life has a purpose," she said. "I'm here to see what it is."

That's why I'd come too, I realized, suddenly riveted by her words. I'd come to get out of my routine, to try a different approach to finding out what was most meaningful to me, to recover from poor choices. Maybe this freak show was exactly what I needed.

Martin gave us our next assignment: "Identify the things about your past and current jobs that you enjoyed," he said. "Then list the things you can no longer tolerate." He told us to create two columns on a piece of paper. Above the left column, we were to write "Like..." and above the other "Dislike..." Then we began to record our observations.

Very quickly a trend emerged. The "Dislike" column grew much faster than the "Like" column. I hated media relations. I was done with hyping products and getting hits. I had also grown tired of the political jockeying for power and the office intrigues that accompanied it. What had once been sport to me—blood sport—had lost its appeal. I was ready to retire from the ring.

The "Like" column contained some surprises. I liked leading creative brainstorming sessions, mentoring younger associates, and public speaking. I began to recognize that I had gifts for facilitating groups, developing strategic plans, and inventing new solutions to business problems. I had never really seen those as abilities before. Maybe I had taken them for granted because they came easily to me.

I was most surprised about my aptitude for people development. When I thought about it, it made some sense. I had probably hired a small army in my ten years in PR. When I wasn't driving them relentlessly to meet goals, I was teaching them to get better at what they did. While my motives were suspect, I was good at helping them improve. Although public speaking was always nerve wracking, I got used to making presentations to clients and new business prospects. And now, ten years on, I realized I was actually quite good at it.

When the day ended, I was exhausted. I dragged myself home. "How was your day?" asked my wife from the kitchen as she prepared dinner. "Any news?"

I was almost incapable of explaining to my wife what had transpired during the day: the unusual participants, the exercises, and the jumble of emotions. It was as though I had entered a parallel universe, one with space aliens who spoke a strange language. Trying to put the experience into words was beyond me.

Underneath the fatigue, I was irritated. Not irritated like you get when your flight is delayed, or you're stuck in traffic, but rather the kind of irritation that accompanies visiting a foreign country, where everything looks similar but is fundamentally different and nothing you do works. There was no guarantee of finding a new vision, and I had only one day left. Maybe the seminar was a colossal waste of time and money. I tossed and turned most of the night, agitated about the looming deadline and dreading the next day.

Dawn came quickly. Again I found myself in the shabby conference room with the self-assured workshop leader. Again he prattled on about "doing well and doing good." Where yesterday I had found his message foreign yet somewhat intriguing, today it was like an air horn at a sporting event. His certainty—that we could envision the life we really wanted—struck me as glib. How could he be so certain? Where was the proof? I was beginning to hate him.

Martin gave us our next assignment: Divide a piece of paper into four sections, one each for Gifts, Talents, Character Qualities, and Contributions. Then we were to list our assets in each of these areas. We were given twenty minutes to work on the inventory in silence. After about five minutes, I had exhausted my list. I had no more than four or five items in each category. I was astonished. I could fill pages with my faults but I struggled with my gifts! Looking around the room I noticed that people were making long, long lists. I felt competitive with the "losers" and judgmental of myself.

My ego was having a hissy fit. I had serious work to do on myself if I was going to discover a new sense of direction. Who was I apart from my role at work? Who was I beyond a fancy title and an expense account? In that moment I had absolutely no idea.

SUFFICIENCY

The mythic hero Theseus, unlike me at the seminar, had one thing going for him when he volunteered for tribute duty and entered the labyrinth: a command of his sufficiency. He trusted that his gifts and talents were well matched for his encounter with the unknown. It was this sense of readiness that enabled him to succeed where others had failed. When he set out from Athens to Crete, he could not have foreseen that he would find the help he needed from Ariadne and Daedalus, but he went anyway.

Whether we know it or not, we too have a formidable array of gifts and talents waiting to be summoned. Like Theseus, we must be confident that they will carry the day under any circumstance, and in any conditions. Our personal resources come in three types: those we are born with, those we develop through experience and practice, and those that only appear in the face of a challenge or in a moment of crisis.

My failure to list my gifts at the workshop revealed a lack of self-awareness, not a lack of gifts. When asked to pay attention to identifying, understanding, and declaring my sufficiency, it proved both edifying and transformational. That inner work only started in earnest when I realized that I could not see what was around the next corner of my life, and that my personal labyrinth could not be solved by following a route that was familiar to me. I needed to challenge myself—and be challenged—to find a new direction.

THE SELF-CRITIC

In Greek myth, the Minotaur was a figure of violence and destruction. He devoured the Athenian tributes sent to the labyrinth so that the blood debt of Athens could be paid. The Minotaur that lives in the labyrinth of our psyche can also be a violent fellow, and the tribute who faces that aggression is ourself. Although we cannot see it, we hear the monster's voice ringing with contempt, seeking to undermine our self-confidence.

This Minotaur is an untethered self-critic. It feeds on doubts and fears about our own adequacy, consuming our gifts and talents as though they were Athenian tributes. With a barrage of negative self-talk, it attempts to undermine our dreams and, worse, our ability to dream them. We can become so mesmerized by this destructive voice that we lose our way and turn against ourselves.

That is precisely what I had been doing. I was involved in acts of self-sabotage. In fact, my internal monologue had turned so negative that it was blocking me from seeing clearly. My problem was not the self-help class, nor the shabby hotel, nor the other participants. Nor was the problem the seminar leader, Martin Rutte. If anything, he was Daedalus. No, they were all convenient scapegoats for the real problem.

True, I had lost my way in the maze of my career, but the real problem was that I had lost myself. Instead of recognizing my gifts, I was firmly focused on my faults. That lack of fair self-talk was a lifelong habit. The trouble at home and work only served to accelerate my negativity.

It is illuminating that Theseus slays the Minotaur with a slash to the throat. With this act, he is symbolically silencing the voice of the self-critic that seeks to rob him of his sufficiency and render him inadequate.

I too needed to take decisive action if I was to silence my Minotaur before it devoured me. By dealing with the self-critic, perhaps I could find my way out of the maze of insufficiency and into the authentic self. I needed to learn how to wield the sword that slays the Minotaur.

{ 7 }

Defeating the Self-Critic

To free us from the expectations of others, to give us back to ourselves—
there lies the great, the singular power of self-respect.

JOAN DIDION

TO WIELD the sword that slays the Minotaur, you must first find it. This mythological metaphor is also practical task. It is our best means of halting the relentless attacks by the self-critic, attacks that sabotage our advance to a more meaningful life. The myth of Theseus helps us locate our vulnerabilities so that we can strengthen them. Faith and trust in our own abilities, the qualities exhibited by Theseus in the labyrinth, are the only way to defeat the monster.

The self-critic is the author of misery. It turns us away from the authentic self and creates a habit of self-abuse. It employs two tactics to lure us further from our heart's guidance and into greater and greater peril. The first is to convince us that it is our best guide, in lockstep with our highest interest. It assures us it will lead us past harm, through the uncertain terrain of our lives, and to a safe haven. We listen intently out of a mistaken notion that we are unable to find and follow our own golden thread through the maze. "Turn left, turn right," coaxes the false friend. "It's not much farther... just around this next corner." The farther we go, the more hopelessly lost and utterly dependent we become. Then the voice turns cruel. "Look how lost you are! You idiot! What's wrong with you? Why can't you ever get it right?"

The second tactic is to remind us we how vulnerable we are to our deficiencies, failings, and mistakes. The self-critic relentlessly broadcasts our faults to an audience of one. These assessments begin with gentle admonitions but grow more malicious with time. Like dispirited hostages, we succumb to the insults of the captor. In this onslaught, our perception of time is altered as well. Instead of setting a course forward to our preferred future, we turn backward to face a distorted past. Selectively chronicling our mistakes for instant replay, the self-critic builds a library of our failures. We stunt our future growth by clinging to our past mistakes.

The price of the self-critic's control is steep. Our hopes and plans shrink and erode. We are on our own case; nothing is ever quite good enough, and an unhealthy addiction to perfection takes root. We begin to shrink from leadership rather than embrace it. We second-guess ourselves, mistrust our instincts, question our knowledge, and undersell our skill. Worse yet, we mistrust the honest intentions and support of others. Even small mistakes—our own or those of others—become fodder for criticism. Satisfaction in a job well done is sacrificed to dwelling on what went wrong. We act as overly critical judge and jury at the same time. We misplace the healthy pride and satisfaction in our accomplishments and affirmations that advance our goals. Like the eagle feasting on the regenerating liver of Prometheus, the self-critic grows ever stronger on a steady diet of our gifts and talents.

THE FIVE ROBBERS

But we don't have to lose ourselves in the critic. We can overcome it. The myth of Theseus proves instructive as a model for how we can silence the critic and embrace our true selves. The story helps us understand the ways we are vulnerable to self-diminishment by depicting five challengers, each representing a different test. Through these challenges, Theseus—our proxy—builds the strength and know-how to face the ultimate confrontation with the Minotaur at the heart of the labyrinth.

Long before his birth, Theseus's father, Aegeus, king of Athens, hid a sword under a great stone. This ancestral object was to be retrieved if and when the boy was strong enough to move the boulder. It took Theseus many years of patient training to gain the strength required to even budge the stone. Finally, when he was eighteen, Theseus removed the stone and claimed the sword. There, buried with the sword, he also found a pair of sandals. This inheritance helped deliver him to his destiny. He would need the sword for his fateful confrontation with the Minotaur. The sandals—the shoes he was destined to fill—made him surefooted on the journey home.

The myth follows Theseus on the road to Athens to meet his father and claim his royal birthright. On his travels Theseus met five robbers who tested both his confidence and courage. By overcoming these challengers, Theseus proved himself capable—he built himself up one step at a time. At the same time, the robbers warn us of the psyche's susceptibility to the self-critic. It is significant that Theseus's challengers were robbers. Stationed

at the entrances to the underworld, these villains were important archetypes. They sought to steal the same treasure from
Theseus they would take from us: confidence in our gifts. Like
Theseus, we must face and defeat them if we are to make the
hero's journey to our own throne of power in the heart.

The first bandit Theseus faced was Periphetes, "the Clubber,"
known for beating his victims into the earth with a brass staff.
This brass club represents the violence we bludgeon ourselves
with. It is a particularly brutal form of self-hatred. This is the
preferred methodology of the inner bully who would dominate
and control us. The Clubber's attacks are relentless. No mistake
is too small to trigger a beating. Judgmental of faults, weaknesses, and failures, the Clubber launches wave after wave of
negativity. Its mission is to beat us down until we have lost all
sense of adequacy. We are left broken and humiliated, defeated
by our own hand. Yet most of us would be horrified by the
thought of treating another person with the ferocity we inflict
on ourselves. Despite its aggression, we are not powerless to
limit the Clubber. Like Theseus, who confronted Periphetes
and used the villain's own brass staff to vanquish him, we can
take steps to disarm the critical voice. First, we must stand our
ground. The Clubber is unused to meeting a strong counterof-
fensive. Recalling all of our positive character traits, abilities,
skills, and successes provides us with a way to counter the
attack. Rather than being focused on getting everything perfect,
our motto must become "Excellence over perfection." A focus
on excellence allows us to hold our lessons as steps toward
a goal rather than setbacks. The Clubber loses ground when
we allow ourselves to continuously improve. Like Theseus, we
build our strength through patience, practice, and the courage
to stand against the tyrant within. But we must choose. Will we
continue to feed the voracious appetite of the critical voice or
engage in fair self-talk? The Clubber is defeated when we take
command of the inner dialogue.

Sinis, "the Bender," liked to tie his victims between two bent pine trees, and then launch them in opposing directions. His victims were, of course, torn apart. The Bender threatens our inner wholeness, a necessity for the journey home. When we are divided against ourselves, we become easy prey. Opposing thoughts and feelings battle for supremacy. We are either on top of the world, or at its bottom. Our thinking is black and white, all or nothing. Our relationships with others are also unstable. Our projections make us see others as either models of perfection or as flawed and fallen, depending on our hypersensitive mood swings. The ability to keep mind, heart, and will in a state of unity is another sword stroke against the critical voice. But what is the binding agent that can ensure wholeness under such divisive pressure? The story of Theseus and Sinis provides a clue: the robber used a rope to entangle his victims. Theseus managed to maintain his footing by refusing to be roped in. When we succumb to inner doubts, second-guessing, or hesitating, we are easily destabilized. By focusing on our highest interests and by being vigilant to the divisive critical voice, we can avoid the lasso of the divided mind. Theseus undid Sinis with his own pine tree catapult. We too can put an end to the divisive voice when we refuse to be ensnared by its siren call.

Sciron, "the Kicker," promised travelers they could pass a narrow land bridge under his control if they knelt and washed his feet. Once they knelt before him, Sciron promptly booted them over the cliff, where they were eaten by a giant turtle. This warns us to guard against subservient and self-diminishing behaviors. Subservience is the inability to stand up for ourselves. When we give our power away, we effectively invite others to boot us headfirst into an abyss of humiliation and shame. We fail to set limits and boundaries in relationships and uphold them with consequences. We allow others to abuse our trust and disrespect our needs. Even our romantic relationships become train wrecks. We choose partners who use, take advantage, lie, cheat, and dominate, all in the name of love. We permit parents, spouses, children, bosses, coworkers, and other relations to tyrannize us. It's our own fault, we tell ourselves. If we could only do more, be better, or anticipate their needs ... In this state of mind—the primitive reptilian brain as represented by the giant turtle—we fail to advocate for ourselves. The need to set limits and boundaries with the self-critic—and in external relationships—is the lesson here. Respecting our own feelings and needs is an act of personal empowerment and a positive first step. Theseus ended Sciron's life by feeding him to the turtle, a reminder that the inner tyrant's dominion is over when we hold our ground, set limits on abusive behavior, and follow through.

Cercyon, "the Wrestler," challenged those passing his kingdom to a wrestling match. The winner got the kingdom, and the loser forfeited his life. Cercyon's cruelty and brute strength were legendary and made him almost impossible to beat. Theseus used strategy and skills, not strength, to defeat the Wrestler. He summoned a combination of gifts and talents—coordination, flexibility, balance, speed, strategy, tactics, and endurance—to defeat Cercyon. In this challenge, the self-critic promotes an inner wrestling match that is rigged against us. When we wrestle with self-doubt, we defeat ourselves. Looking backward, becoming mired in regret, keeps us from moving forward. We become exhausted, sapped of our strength. The same holds true for fretting about the future, which is beyond our control. Theseus's example teaches us to seize the present moment in order to command our inherent gifts and our accrued knowledge, skills, and experience. Remembering and applying our skills in the moment of the challenge can defeat the critical voice within, even when its strength appears overpowering.

Procrustes was the final bandit. Known as "the Stretcher," he operated a lethal bed-and-breakfast for unsuspecting guests. Procrustes had only two sizes of bed. He guaranteed that whatever your size, the bed he selected for you would fit perfectly. Too short? He would stretch you until you fit. Too long? He would literally cut you down to size. The Stretcher met his match in Theseus, who settled the matter by permanently right-sizing the thief. Theseus decapitated him and cut off his feet using Procrustes's own axe. This encounter teaches us to beware of measuring ourselves against others. Where do we feel like we are too little or too much in our lives? The need to be better than others, or feeling inferior, signals an unhealthy relationship with the self. The encounter with the Stretcher also warns us about the need to fit in, and the need for acceptance and approval. We must accept and approve of ourselves without requiring the validation of others as the basis for self-worth.

SELF-WORTH

Despite his exploits, Theseus was no superhero. He was only a demigod. To assume we need to be more than who we are robs us of our power, hindering our ability to defeat the self-critic. In fact, those thoughts are the thoughts of the self-critic itself— "I'm not strong enough, skilled enough, prepared enough." What made Theseus extraordinary was his willingness to face the challenges as himself. In each instance he stayed true to a singular commitment, a commitment we can make as well: to honor our self-worth. Self-worth is an appreciation of one's own value. Neither vainglorious nor overly meek, self-worth enables quiet confidence. The three aspects of self-worth, according to author Angeles Arrien, are self-love, self-trust, and self-respect.[1]

Self-love means that we have a healthy level of affection and compassion for ourselves. We are not overly harsh or critical of our abilities, and although we are always striving to be and do our best, we allow ourselves to learn from mistakes. The key to self-love is accepting we are enough, a concept Angeles Arrien refers to as "original medicine." In her book *The Four-Fold Way* she states,

> Many indigenous societies believe that we all possess "original medicine": personal power, duplicated nowhere else on the planet. No two individuals carry the same combination of talents or challenges; therefore, when we compare ourselves to others, native peoples see this as a sign that we do not believe that we have original medicine.[2]

Self-love enables us to see our gifts as a birthright. Like Theseus, our challenge is to find the place where our treasures reside. That place is represented in the myth by a stone marker that simultaneously conceals, protects, and challenges. In the myth of Theseus, the stone marked the location of buried gifts and was a test of strength and resolve. We too must take up the challenge to find and claim our gifts. This can only be accomplished by befriending ourselves, by reflecting, and by seeking to understand what makes us truly unique.

Claiming our positive gifts, talents, and character qualities, as well as our contributions to relationships, work, the community, and the wider world is an act of self-love. One concrete way to begin a practice of self-love is to start a daily journal. Identifying and recording the gifts applied during the day, the positive impact those gifts created, and the outcomes that resulted anchors the practice. Like the stone that marked the place of Theseus's inheritance, recognizing all that is working in our nature can shift our focus from self-diminishment to positive self-talk.

Self-trust means we have confidence in our own abilities. Like Theseus, we must learn to trust that we can meet and respond to the opportunities and challenges that occur on our life's journey. We must also learn to trust that our gifts and resourcefulness will carry the day. The word "learn" is operative. Self-trust grows as a result of facing and overcoming tests,

challenges, and adversity. Through such difficulties we are ini-
tiated into deeper levels of faith in ourselves. Such tests also
uncover hidden gifts, gifts that are concealed until the moment
they are most needed or have been earned. They are like the sandals that Theseus found along with the sword, an unexpected
reward for bravery and commitment. Meeting and overcoming inner and outer challenges earn us the confidence to step
into our destiny as well. As self-trust grows, we can better face
the unfamiliar circumstances on our own journey of meaning, knowing that we can handle whatever happens. Through
our own labors, we come to recognize the folly of taking our
direction from the self-critic instead of following the golden
thread of self-trust. The self-critic misleads us through fear and
rebuke; self-trust leads us through encouragement and affir-
mation. "We have all a better guide in ourselves, if we would
attend to it, than any other person can be," wrote Jane Austen
in *Mansfield Park*.[3] Self-trust is the practice of affirming the voice
of that inner guide, a voice that grows stronger with conscious
and consistent attention.

Self-respect is the belief in our own worth and dignity. We
value ourselves but never from a place of unhealthy pride or
conceit. We can celebrate our accomplishments and provide a
fair and honest assessment of our mistakes for the purpose of
continuous improvement. When we have a healthy regard for
ourselves, there is no need to brag about accomplishments or
to be jealous or comparative of others. We stop depending on
others to make us feel good about ourselves, and we stop allowing their opinions to diminish us. We take full responsibility for
our thoughts and feelings.

The sword of Theseus is the symbol associated with this
quality. It represents a commitment to self-responsibility. We do
not see ourselves as victims but as the authors of our own lives.
The sword reminds us to cut out clubbing, bending, kicking,

wrestling, or stretching self-talk. Like Theseus in his encounters with the robbers, we must stand up for ourselves against the self-critic, and set limits and boundaries to prevent it from consuming us. Ultimately, we must use the blade of self-respect in our battle with the robbers. While we might never completely silence the self-critic, we can manage it effectively. Like Theseus, we too can overcome the challengers that stand between destiny and us.

{ 8 }

Uncertainty

Creativity requires the courage to let go of certainty.

ERICH FROMM

HEN THE Success Factor program ended, I was almost certain I hadn't gotten it. I was no Saul on the road to Damascus radically altered by a flash of light. Nor was I Siddhartha enlightened under the Bodhi tree. It appeared I had gotten on the slow train to transformation, lurching forward and back, huffing and puffing as it inched toward a horizon that never seemed to get any closer. I was impatient. I wanted instant gratification, a clear sense of direction, and assurances of my success. Of course the Success Factor hadn't provided any assurances. There was no miracle. Just more work. Despite the lack of epiphany, I had made a few critical decisions.

The course had helped me reach a conclusion. Not only was I finished with the public relations business, but I was also finished with working for someone else. Something inside me had snapped at my last performance review. I could no longer tolerate taking orders from other people. I was no longer willing to be a good soldier killing myself to advance someone else's ambitions and build someone else's fortune. And I certainly wasn't about to let them fire me for doing their dirty work. No sir, I wanted to be my own boss. That would take money, a tangible idea about how to make money, and a source of said money in the form of clients or customers. At present, I had none of the above.

Secondly, I had a premonition. The workshop leader, Martin Rutte, was quite effective. I was intrigued by his ability to think on his feet and confront people with new possibilities for their life and work. He was one of the best questioners I had ever met. His questions were disarming and disorienting at the same time. They took you to an unfamiliar place, a place where you couldn't look at your life in the same old way. It was a little irritating being asked to reexamine what you took for granted, but it was also therapeutic. I began to wonder if I could do what Martin did.

Finally, I saw the need to embrace uncertainty. To be "self-made," I had to leave my comfort zone and journey into unknown territory. While the PR agency was anything but comfortable, it was known territory, familiar. Despite the horrible environment, I had clients and a steady income, and I knew the game. Job security can be a bit like prison. You get your three squares, and you learn to adjust to the routine and navigate the politics. I realized that I had become institutionalized in the ten years I spent working for a paycheck. I worried that I had become a "lifer," ill equipped for the outside, where there was no safety net and no guarantee of success. That was a different kind of pressure than flogging media hits and putting bums in seats at press events for clients.

Successful entrepreneurs thrive on uncertainty. I knew that from my work with clients who ran their own businesses, clients who had started from nothing and built their companies into robust enterprises. They did not seem to want or need the kind of assurances I was seeking. Mavericks all, they trusted themselves, made their own decisions, and lived with the consequences both good and bad. Uncertainty for an entrepreneur was an adventure to be enjoyed. To me, it felt like a penalty to be suffered. I needed a self-administered attitudinal adjustment. In other words, I needed a swift kick.

RISK TOLERANCE

Risk tolerance, a common term in the investment industry, refers to one's ability to stomach potential market swings that affect the value of an asset and/or portfolio of stocks. The return on investment is often in proportion to the risk involved. Low risk usually means small returns. Bigger risks can mean a jackpot—or a crash landing. I knew myself well enough to recognize that a low-risk, low-return solution was not my destiny. I also knew that I needed to find a high-return solution and fast. I had been around long enough, and seen enough people come and go, to know that the agency had already fired me. They just hadn't told me when I was leaving. It might be two weeks, two months, or two years, but they were finished with me. I needed to face reality head on rather than play peek-a-boo.

Two years later, I would come across a quote from Peter Senge's *The Fifth Discipline* that stuck with me:

> The gap between vision and current reality is also a source of energy. If there was no gap, there would be no need for any action to move toward the vision...We call this gap *creative tension*.[1]

That notion—creative tension—perfectly summarized what I was feeling at the time. But despite the anxiety, there wasn't enough creative tension to bring about change. The goal of leaving the agency within the year was too vague—it lacked specificity—and this vagueness was causing mission creep. I watched the weeks pass, waiting for a great cosmic light bulb to switch on, illuminating my next step. And what if it didn't light? Would I continue to push my departure date further and further out to compensate?

My "stuckness" was like quicksand. The more I struggled to get out, the more I sank. I began to see that it was rooted in a powerful belief: "You must have everything figured out in advance!" The need for certainty and control, my fear of making a misstep or failing, was arresting my progress. Waiting for a master plan prevented me from getting traction and moving forward. Drifting along, waiting for enlightenment, was getting me nowhere. It was increasing my anxiety rather than producing creative tension. Instead, maybe I just needed to take one step, and then the next, and the next? The idea of taking action rather than waiting for the perfect plan and the right circumstances turned out to be the way forward.

The only way I could get "unstuck" was to commit to a positive next step. That step had to be specific and measurable. Only a goal like that, I reckoned, would compel me to act. The Chinese have a saying about this: "When your cart reaches the foot of the mountain, a path will appear." It is a reminder that vision is often relative. From a long distance, it may appear that there is no path forward. When we are too close to something, we may also lose our way.

I set a drop-dead date for my departure. May fifth was my birthday. It was ten months away. I decided it was as good a day as any to begin life as an entrepreneur. But whenever I thought about leaving without a firm plan in place, without some guarantee of success, my stomach churned. I had family responsibilities, and the rent and bills to pay. It was hard in those moments to remember the richness of my personal resources. And it was especially hard to manage the critical voice within. As I faced the May fifth deadline, the self-critic seemed to take great delight in fanning the flames of fear and increasing my sense of helplessness. I needed to find a way to fight back.

Theseus found the strength and the tools that helped him fight the robbers under a stone marker. If it worked for Theseus, I reasoned, it could work for me. I decided to work with a stone of my own. I found one during a walk one day. It fit perfectly into the palm of my hand—small enough to be invisible to others yet large enough to do its work. I began to carry it with me everywhere. Every time the inner critic tried to rob me of my sense of sufficiency, I would squeeze the stone hard and fight back. I reminded myself that I had what it took to figure things out. In silence, I recited the list of my gifts and talents. That inventory had grown since the workshop. I added to it regularly. The more I repeated the list, the more ridiculous the voice of my fears became. I had discovered I had an arsenal at my disposal. My gifts, talents, character qualities, and other resources far outnumbered the fears.

Something else was required to fight my fear and conquer the maze. Pessimism and resignation were weakening my resolve. I had to drop the idea that the future was the Minotaur waiting to devour me. Instead, I started to tell myself the future was my friend. Being optimistic and believing firmly in the best possible outcome is the mind-set of an entrepreneur. In order to be one, I needed to start to think like one. That attitude had carried the day for Theseus. I had to trust it would carry the day for me too.

{ 9 }

Gestation

---

*Everything is gestation and then birthing. To let each impression
and each embryo of a feeling come to completion, entirely in itself, in
the dark, in the unsayable, the unconscious, beyond the reach of one's
own understanding, and with deep humility and patience to wait for
the hour when a new clarity is born: this alone is what it means
to live as an artist: in understanding as in creating.*

RAINER MARIA RILKE

W E BOUGHT a home with the help of my in-laws.
Our little family moved from the apartment on
the hill that overlooked the park to a little red
brick semidetached house in a residential neighborhood in
Toronto's west end. Lynne was pregnant again, and when she
wasn't throwing up, she was elated about having another baby.

I was excited too. Having a family was the only long-term vision I had for my life. However, the combination of the move, mortgage payments, another child on the way, and the uncertainty of my career rocketed my stress level into the stratosphere. Part of me wanted to shelve my quest for a new career and wait for a more convenient, less anxious time. But that was mere wishful thinking. I knew that I could not afford the luxury of postponing my search. I had to face my situation head on and deal with it even with monumental changes taking place at home.

In Greek myth there is a three-headed dog, Cerberus, who stands on guard at the entrance to the underworld. Cerberus's job is to let you into Hades but prevent you from ever leaving, perhaps like the clerk at the Hotel California. One head of the dog represents the past, the second the present, and the third the future. To my mind, it felt like my job had its own three-headed dog stationed at the exit. The head of the past seemed intent on having me only look backward. "You don't know how to do anything else. Stick to your knitting," it growled. The second head was intent on entrapping me in deadlines, overwork, and worry. "Too much on your plate already," it said, panting. The third head was committed to having me chase my tail. "You can't see what's next, so you can't act. You're stuck here!" it howled over and over.

Meanwhile, the underworld of the agency felt more dysfunctional by the day. Rival account groups seemed as menacing to me as street gangs. Enmity between offices was straining interoffice cooperation to a breaking point. While the second head of the dog was keeping me busy dealing with conflict after conflict, my enemies were plotting. They could smell my blood. People may not have known the details of my last performance review, but everyone knew I was on the hit list. I'd become a target.

It always seemed like bad timing when the agency's New York–based human resources group scheduled a management training session for our office. The previous program they ran in Toronto was a disaster. It was a strategy course, led by a burned-out corporate vice-president, a codger in his sixties. He had been put out to pasture, dumped into a personnel role when he was no longer fit to do client work. The man was shaking so badly at the beginning of the workshop we couldn't tell if he was nervous, needed a drink, or both. Maybe it was body wisdom. He could probably sense this was a nest of vipers. Rather than waste billable time, we struck instantly by engaging him in a debate about the difference between a goal, an objective, and a strategy. It was a question we employed routinely to terrorize junior account executives. If he'd known the answer coming in to the day, he certainly didn't on his way out.

This time around was a little different. The top account directors from across the country had been assembled, like Mob bosses, in a hotel meeting room. The workshop topic was "Supervisory Skills." Unlike the last guy they sent into our snake pit, Joel, the workshop leader, was a pro. He had a no-nonsense presence about him, the demeanor of a combat veteran. There was a crispness to how he presented himself. With his close-cropped hair, unwrinkled white shirt, gray flannels, and blue blazer, Joel had the bearing of someone in charge.

Hired by the company to train its managers internationally, he tried to engage the twenty of us in a series of exercises and assignments. He was met with a mixture of irritation from those on client deadlines and resignation from those who had given up hope of positive change. The rest were measuring him, waiting to strike. None of it fazed him a bit.

Sensing our obstinacy, Joel switched gears. He began to tell a story about a donkey in a pit. "There's this donkey," he started, like Al Pacino revving up a monologue. "It falls in this pit, braying away until a guy shows up." Joel was now like a snake charmer charming the snakes. He used the story like a flute to induce a kind of trance state.

"The guy's name is Eddie, Eddie from Queens. He's been around, so he decides the best thing to do is get rid of the body. Eddie knows something about this, since he's done it before under other circumstances, which we can't go into."

Now everyone in the meeting room was immersed in the plight of the donkey. The irritated ones, the hopeless ones, and the hit men had all been transformed into wide-eyed kids.

"Eddie gets this shovel," Joel continued. "He starts throwing dirt on the donkey, filling the pit." Joel paused for a sip of water. He was enjoying himself.

"The donkey finally gets what's going on. He shuts up. Eddie's so busy shoveling, he doesn't realize the donkey's got a plan. The donkey shakes off each shovelful of dirt and steps up. He steps up and up and up. Eventually the pile of dirt is so high the donkey is able to jump out of the pit and run off."

Joel paused again, letting the message sink in. "You guys seem like you're in a pit to me. Only you're getting buried. Lets talk about getting out, stepping up."

I was fascinated by how Joel had used a story to shift the mood in the room. Instantly, he was able to reveal a common issue, something we were all struggling with. He also seemed to offer a solution, though a cryptic one. It was like seeing the Flying Wallendas walking a tightrope in high winds, or hearing Clarence Darrow charming a biased jury. It was exhilarating.

I don't know what prompted Joel to speak to me at a break. Maybe it was exasperation, or maybe he sensed my fascination with his skill. "What's wrong with these people?" he asked with concern.

"You're in a war zone," I said. "It's always been this way. Lately, it's gotten much worse."

"What do you suggest we do to improve the condition?" he asked.

"Pray," I said.

I went home at the end of the day thinking about Joel's question. What would I do? The problem ran deep. It was in the walls; it permeated the culture. When I first arrived at the agency, the CEO (dead Keith Richards) informed me I would never succeed unless I changed my style. I was way too nice. "You'll never last around here unless your people are more scared of you than they are of the client or the media, so toughen up, mate!" he said with cheerful menace.

I didn't have to be told twice. While the top executives gave a pretense of camaraderie, they were cutthroat with their teams, their clients, and each other. It was how we were expected to act—strength, aggression, and malice. We trained our teams to behave accordingly. Of course, publicly they espoused the platitude of "We're all in this together." But the real values were: "Everyone for themselves." We learned those lessons well. If you didn't, you were buried alive.

I began to understand the impact that leadership has on an organization's culture. If the boss values unity of purpose and collaboration, there's a much better chance it will permeate the organization. If the style is divide and conquer, dysfunctional behavior will prevail. Our executives were of the divide and conquer breed, a philosophy that revealed itself the very next day.

Joel asked the current CEO—Keith Richards's protégée—to attend the second day of the workshop. He hoped her attendance might facilitate conflict resolution. What he didn't know was that the CEO was the most feared person in the organization. She was the queen cobra, with the uncanny ability to mesmerize her victims and strike instantly to get what she wanted. From observing her closely over the years, I knew she was most dangerous when coiled and inscrutable. I had watched her reduce grown men to tears, even clients, and devour her rivals one by one.

There she sat, a cobra surrounded by prey. The tension in the meeting room was thick.

Joel asked the group to describe the biggest challenge managers were having at the agency. No one said a word. He reminded us of our dialogue from the previous day. "Trust?" he asked. A few people nodded. The CEO remained silent, likely choosing who would be her appetizer.

"Why don't we set some ground rules for this conversation?" Joel suggested. "Trust is hard to talk about. Especially when you're the donkey in the pit. What guarantees would help everyone talk openly about the problems?"

"Immunity," I said.

Joel turned to the Cobra. "Yes?" he asked.

"Yes," she said stone-faced.

"Good. Let's break into small groups," he suggested, "and talk about what makes trust difficult."

For the next thirty minutes, the small groups explored the agency culture, a culture everyone professed to hate but felt powerless to change. At the end of the time allotment, Joel asked each group to report their findings. The problems identified were predictably uniform: overwork, ruthlessness, and infighting. The solutions from each group, however, were vague. That was also predictable. No one believed change would happen.

Behind her lidless gaze, I knew the CEO was pissed. She said all the right things about fresh starts and the need to work together on solutions. But she was a PR professional. Like the rest of us, she was a highly compensated professional liar. I left the meeting room searching for the bathroom. The CEO was waiting at the elevator, obviously annoyed by her captivity. "If I had wanted to spend my time dealing with people issues, I would have gone into HR," she hissed, as the doors slid shut.

At the end of the day, I approached Joel. "That didn't solve anything," I said. "It may even have made things worse."

He considered my assessment. "It was witnessed," he said. "That makes a difference. I'll be asked for a report by New York. My advice to you is to make like a donkey. Step up and step out."

STEP UP, STEP OUT

The next morning I boarded a flight for the West to see a client we had paired with an emerging amateur sport, freestyle skiing. It was a sexy sponsorship that was good marketing for a dull product. I was headed to negotiate a deal with a venue in Calgary to host an international competition. The sponsorship was a win-win-win: the client had a sports property that added vitality and interest to his brand. The amateur athletes finally had stable financial backing and some marketing muscle to showcase their sport. The agency was making a tidy profit managing and promoting the tie-in. It made everyone happy, including me. The project—part of a much larger account run by another team at the agency—was a bright spot. The client was a smart marketer and a nice guy, the athletes were a breath of fresh air, and I got out of head office.

The plane was only half full, good news given I was traveling in economy. As I settled into an aisle seat, I couldn't stop thinking about the training session the previous day. The agency was a sweatshop that chewed people up, spit them out, and destroyed their values in the process. But it was effective. Like in a law firm, profits came from driving everybody to bill as many hours as possible. You started early, stayed late, and worked weekends. You called staff back from vacation, got them off their sickbed, made them miss their kid's concert—whatever it took to achieve your billing targets.

Personally, I had been raked over the coals twice when my billing dropped: first when my father-in-law died, and again when my daughter was born.

In the agency model, people were disposable. You shov-
eled as much dirt on their backs as they could manage, and
then you buried them. Like Eddie, I had been shoveling and
shoveling without question, barely looking up from the dirty
work. Unfortunately, I wasn't even as smart as a donkey. It
wasn't until I was almost buried by the guy shoveling dirt on
me that I noticed something was wrong. Joel's story made me
contemplate what stepping up might look like. Was it possible
to deliver success and maintain human values and goodwill? I
wondered if a company predicated on those values would perform better in the long term.

There's an old Turkish proverb that says, "No matter how
far you have gone on a wrong road, turn back." I couldn't undo
what I had done at the agency. I couldn't wipe away the damage
I'd done to others and myself. But maybe I could still find that
right road. I thought about Joel's advice. What did it mean to
step up and step out?

One thing was certain. I was no longer willing to be either
the donkey in the pit or the guy with the shovel. I had been both.
Burying my values and humanity for the sake of a buck was no
longer worth the cost. I had seen my future in that meeting
room, and it crawled on its belly. There had to be a better, more
upright, way to work.

I arrived in Calgary and settled into a downtown hotel. The
following day, my client and I made our way to the sports complex. The venue officials were quite excited about hosting an
international tour event at their site. We finalized details and
settled the matter with a handshake. My client was elated. "Let's
have dinner," he said in the cab.

We ordered a good bottle of wine and a fine meal. It was a
ritual we both enjoyed when traveling on sponsorship business.
We discussed the event we were planning, the marketing opportunity, and potential television partners. We also discussed

which athletes we would profile and how we would make them household names. Finally, after a lot of wine, the conversation turned to the future.

"What do you want to do when you grow up?," the client asked.

"Have my own business," I said in a knee-jerk response.

"Let me know when you do that," he responded, pouring himself the remainder of the wine. "I'd like to work with you."

{ 10 }

Escape Artist

The object of life is not to be on the side of the majority, but to escape finding oneself in the ranks of the insane.

MARCUS AURELIUS

I COULDN'T SLEEP thinking about the possibility of escaping hell. I tossed and turned, filled with a kind of electric nervousness. The door I had dreamed about seemed suddenly within reach, almost at my fingertips. The thought of opening it, however, was exhilarating one moment and terrifying the next. I was having a hard time catching my breath. I replayed my client's words over and over in my mind, trying to reassure myself I had actually heard them. "I'd like to work with you."

Unsettled, I could remain in bed no longer. I dressed and went down to the lobby looking for coffee. It was the middle of the night. The hotel was empty. I wandered into the equally empty restaurant and sat at the same table where I'd been with my client just a few short hours earlier. There, I searched for a clue, some material evidence that the conversation had indeed taken place. There was nothing to confirm the event, to validate my recollection. The table had been cleared, the tablecloth changed, the silverware reset for breakfast. Maybe I'd misunderstood. Maybe he hadn't said it at all. Maybe he was just being friendly and supportive. Maybe he was drunk. Maybe he wouldn't remember. He'd made no commitment; there were no promises. His words were probably just friendly encouragement. He was a good guy being a good guy.

But what if he did mean it? I would finally be able to leave the agency—leave before they threw me out. I could start something of my own, something good. Working with amateur athletes and a great client might be a launching pad for a whole new business. Helping young athletes succeed was a hell of a lot more appealing than pitching media types about the benefits of using gelatin products as plant food. Helping put a hero on the winner's podium at the Albertville Olympics in France was more meaningful than waging the cola wars or promoting the dubious advantages of aspartame.

Would I go back to the office in Toronto and resign? Would I hang out a shingle? Would I invite some of my current team to come on the adventure of a lifetime? Or would I continue to fret about plunging my family, my teammates, and myself into peril? Cerberus, the three-headed dog, barked and barked.

BREAKING OUT

Every successful jailbreak requires three things: a desperate need to be free, an assessment of the weaknesses of the prison system, and an escape plan. Prisons have doors, windows, and ventilation systems that can be breached if you are willing to risk it. Tunnels can be dug, fences scaled, guards bribed, and keys stolen. It helps if you leave under the cover of darkness, have some knowledge of the territory outside the prison walls, and set up a good getaway vehicle. A confederate on the outside is helpful too.

The prison where I was languishing was not made of bricks and mortar. Yet it seemed as secure as Guantanamo Bay. I was a prisoner of my mental models, the assumptions and beliefs that were like iron bars on the windows of my outlook. I had never worked for myself, always been an employee. While I had been creative in that role, I had been functioning within a predetermined system. I had a boss, an office, colleagues, and clients. I knew what to expect. I would have none of that out on my own; there would be no safety net. Even though the cell door seemed to be unlocked, and open, I wasn't sure I had the courage to escape. Just thinking about taking that leap made me feel queasy. Lynne was entering her final trimester. Could I start a business and feed a family of four? Integrating an infant into a busy household was exhausting work. Maybe I didn't have the energy or the guts to leave. Maybe I couldn't make the transformation from "good account guy" to entrepreneur. I currently worked for the largest, most powerful PR agency in the world. If I left, I would forfeit my salary, perks, three-week vacation, and pension.

Over the years, I had seen a lot of people leave to start their own businesses. Most of them never seemed to amount to much. They had a few clients and hung out at the PR society events, drinking too much and talking up "old friends" who barely gave them the time of day. They were visible for a year, maybe two, before they drowned in the sea of an indifferent marketplace. Others had taken corporate jobs, or moved to the civil service or the media. None of that appealed to me in the least. Those careers seemed claustrophobic, like different cells in the same cellblock. If I was going to break out of hell, I needed to get on with it. George Bernard Shaw identifies the challenge:

> The open mind never acts: when we have done our utmost to arrive at a reasonable conclusion, we still ... must close our minds for the moment with a snap, and act dogmatically on our conclusions.[1]

In order to "act dogmatically," I needed to commit once and for all. I could see that the open door would not remain open by itself, or for long. I had to be opportunistic and walk through it. But first, I needed to throttle a dog.

THE TWELFTH LABOR OF HERCULES

Hercules, most famous of the Greek heroes, got in a lot of hot water for the murder of his wife and children. He pleaded insanity, blaming Hera, the goddess of women and marriage. Even then, men were blaming women for their deeds.

Unsurprisingly, he was found guilty as charged and was sentenced to perform a series of impossible labors, as difficult as they were dangerous. King Eurystheus was appointed Hercules's taskmaster. Skinning lions, killing hydras, mucking filth from enormous stables in a single day, or poaching cattle from a fiend were much less difficult than the twelfth labor. For his twelfth and final labor, Hercules was ordered to fetch the monster dog Cerberus from Hades. He agreed to capture Cerberus without the use of weapons and without harming him.

Hercules managed to overpower Cerberus by grabbing him by the throat. This is a metaphor that instructs us about how to silence three negative inner voices:

- The voice of the past that is intent on having us only look backward. This is the voice that growls, "Shoulda, woulda, coulda!"

- The voice that has us obsessing about deadlines, overwork, and worry about what's on our plate. "Too much to do; so little time."
- The voice that ignites fear about what lies waiting for us around the next corner. "What if, what if, what if?"

We can learn much from Hercules about defeating the three-headed dog and gaining freedom from self-inflicted fear and misery.

THE PAST

Hercules wisely consulted the old Eleusinian mysteries for the secrets of the underworld before departing to Hades. No human had ever returned, let alone survived, a visit. These teachings provided important guidance for Hercules in his quest to defeat Cerberus and complete the twelfth of his epic labors.

When we use the past as a source of wisdom, we too can defeat Cerberus and escape hell. Recalling memories, examples, and stories of past success reminds us of our competence. Gathering wisdom from those who have demonstrated courage, resourcefulness, and proactivity is instructive to our own lives.

The past can also be a trap. When we become overly mired in the status quo or tied to our comfort zone, we become stuck in old ways of thinking and doing things. This prevents continuous learning and renewal. Decay sets in. We lose the ability to be innovative and progressive. Meanwhile, the wheel of time is turning. Life is changing around us, and we lose our ability to meet challenges with confidence.

THE PRESENT

Hercules was able to defeat the three-headed dog because he was sufficient to the task. He was not arrested by fear of Cerberus's ferocious appearance or reputation. Nor was he overly worried about what might befall him in his encounter with this difficult customer—a beast with three monstrous heads, the tail of a dragon, and a back covered with poisonous vipers.

The time to act is here and now. When we are present and ready to seize the moment, we can respond with all of our faculties and resources. This "sufficiency" enables our success. We do not allow ourselves to be distracted or divided over what might happen. When we face the present moment like Hercules and meet difficulties and challenges with courage and resourcefulness, we carry the day.

The present, however, can be a place of dangerous velocity, inefficiency, and overwhelm. Too many people chase their tails rather than focus on heartfelt action. Putting out fires and dealing with social and professional snake pits can take up so much of our time that there is little left for real work.

THE FUTURE

When we see the future as a friend and not a force bent on destroying us, we meet it with optimism. Optimism always carries its own weather system—adventure, excitement, and unlimited possibility. We need such winds to make transitions from our current circumstances to our preferred future.

Despite the odds, Hercules did not waver in his belief that he would prevail in his encounter with Cerberus. He prepared well and anticipated his own victory by planning the return from the underworld across the river Styx. Hercules promised Hades, the god of the underworld, that he would not harm Cerberus. By this agreement, Hercules was permitted to carry out his mission and bring the three-headed dog back to the middle world.

It is important to recognize that Cerberus was not defeated by lethal force. He was defeated by a firm hand. When we use the harsh critic to beat ourselves down, we are diminished; we are defeated well before the encounter with Cerberus. The confidence and resiliency to meet the challenge has been lost to negative self-talk.

Cerberus is a difficult challenger, but he can be overcome if we are courageous and resourceful. The past, present, and future, when managed well, support wise action. Informed by the past and optimistic about the future, we are called by the present moment to face our fears and follow our hearts.

DECISION POINT

The morning arrived at last. I met my client for breakfast. He said nothing about our conversation the previous evening. Making small talk, we finished our meal and then took a cab through the city to the airport.

As we boarded the flight back to Toronto I said, "I've been thinking about our talk last night. I really appreciate your encouragement. You know, I believe I could be ready to open an agency of my own in six weeks. I'd like to pitch for your business."

{ 11 }

Departure

There is a time for departure even when there's no certain place to go.

TENNESSEE WILLIAMS

I HAD JUST resigned. The Cobra sat across from me holding the letter. She was considering her next play. She acted friendly, benevolent, encouraging. Her geniality was an obvious ploy to gain information. She hadn't seen this coming. "Are you going to take the freestyle account?" she asked.

It was my turn to be stunned. "I don't know," I said. It was the truth. There was no deal in place, no guarantee. The client had been surprised at the news I was going to start my own business and do it almost immediately. I had suggested it could be up and running in six weeks, the time frame picked from the ether. He had wished me luck, smiled, and disappeared into the business class cabin. I had found my seat in economy and begun to formulate a plan.

The only part of the plan I was willing to share with the Cobra was the departure date. "I'm prepared to give you one month's notice," I said. "That will allow an orderly transition of all my accounts." I half expected she would waive the offer and give me the boot on the spot.

The Cobra's eyes narrowed. "That will be sufficient," she replied, licking her lips. She obviously wanted to constrain me long enough to plot. Better to keep me where she could see me until she figured out my intentions. She also knew it would impede my ability to advance any plans. "Taking any account staff with you?" she asked in an offhand way.

"I don't know," I said. "I haven't thought about it." That was a half-truth. In fact, I had thought about nothing else on my way back from Calgary. It wasn't a current employee that I was hoping to recruit. It was someone who had worked for me previously, someone who had left the agency to move west with her new husband.

Elinor had started as my secretary. Over the years, she had risen through the ranks to become one of the best account executives at the agency. She was my right hand before she left and the architect of the freestyle sponsorship. She had found a perfect match for the client after analyzing every amateur winter sport organization in the country. I needed her help if I was to have any hope of succeeding on my own. She was a logistical genius. The big obstacle now was location. She was in Edmonton. Would she come back to Toronto? Her husband had a good job in telecommunications. How would that work, I wondered.

As I left the Cobra's office, I happened to glance back. She was studying me on my way out the door with a look I had seen many times. She was calculating where to place the knife to ensure the slowest and most agonizing death possible.

That evening I phoned Elinor. She made me recount the conversation word for word. "Wow! I can't believe you finally did it," she said. "I would've given anything to see the look on her face. Now what are you going to do?"

"I'm going to pursue the sponsorship account," I replied. "The client made no promises, but I think I can pry some of that business loose. We created it, and we know where it needs to go next."

"Whaddaya mean 'we'?" she asked.

"I need your help," I replied.

"In case you've forgotten, I'm 2,200 miles away," she exclaimed.

"That's just logistics. Are you in or not?"

"You're such a jerk! I can't give you an answer on the spot. I can help you long distance, but I can't promise any more than that. I have family obligations."

"Look, this is a ground floor opportunity—once in a lifetime," I said, selling hard. "We can be business partners."

"I don't want to be business partners. That's too much responsibility, not to mention liability. And you're a pain in the ass to work with."

"At the very least, I need you here to help me develop a pitch for the business," I said. "But I can't do that until I get out of here in a couple of weeks."

"I'll think about it," she replied. "I need to talk to my husband."

PERSONA NON GRATA

There are certain periods in your life when time goes by so fast it's dizzying, but the four-week notice period was not one of them. It seemed to stretch on forever. Each day I went into the office at 9:00 a.m. I closed my door and emerged at 5:00 p.m., and returned home. There were surprisingly few meetings, even fewer phone calls, and no colleagues stopping in to chat. I was persona non grata, a dead man walking. Account plans had already been made for the year ahead and team members assigned to run day-to-day business. It was business as usual. My imminent departure caused barely a blip.

Predictably, the Cobra was not going to allow me access to any client contacts. That was too risky. She would inform them of my departure after it happened. I knew the drill. "We thank him for his contribution . . . wish him well . . . etcetera, etcetera." I'd seen it play out countless times over the years. I also knew in my bones she was planning something. I could sense it.

My days were spent in self-imposed solitary confinement, with lots of time to contemplate the leap I would make into the abyss. If Elinor declined to help me, I would be doing it alone and without a safety net. You could bet the Cobra would be moving heaven and earth to shore up the freestyle account. That's what I would do in her shoes. But she was up to something, something I couldn't put my finger on. Samuel Johnson suggests times of peril are the perfect medium for insight: "When a man knows he is to be hanged in a fortnight, it concentrates his mind wonderfully," he wrote.[1]

I was concentrating on exiting in a month without incident. I needed to figure out how to earn some money fast so that I could pay my bills. If making the decision to leave was scary, being between the worlds was making me even more anxious. I developed a stiff neck from worrying.

THE TWINS

Evenings at home were filled with childcare responsibilities and preparations for the pending arrival of our second baby. If Lynne was freaked out about the convergence of two major life changes, she didn't betray it. She was deeply immersed in her own preparations for birth, both physical and emotional. We had no illusions about what would happen with the workload at home. As one bleary-eyed neighbor said after the arrival of his second child, "One child is none. Two is twenty."

Lynne was starting maternity leave shortly. We would need to survive on her maternity benefits and some vacation pay. There would be no other money coming into the house.

My parents seemed excited about the new baby and less enthusiastic about my plans. In retrospect, it was probably hard for them not to question aloud what they must have viewed as recklessness. They were not big risk takers, though my father liked to play small-stakes poker from time to time. He had been a company man, she a stay-at-home mom. They were both children of the Great Depression and came of age during the Second World War. My dad, fatherless by age eleven, never finished high school. My mother, the child of an alcoholic, was chronically ill, in and out of hospitals with lupus most of her adult life. Despite the obstacles, they had built a solid life—built it with their own hands. My father had risen to vice-president of sales at a pharmaceutical company. Like many others of their generation, safety and stability remained important values for my parents. In their day, you didn't dare gamble with a good job; you might not find another. Now their son was rolling the dice at the worst possible time, a time when everything could come tumbling down. Could I go to them for financial help? I could, but I didn't want to involve them. I had never wanted or asked for help like that in past.

Few entrepreneurs live as hermits. Business decisions are life decisions and vice versa. Most small businesses are family businesses, and everyone in the family has a stake in their success or failure. When a business is finding its feet, everyone has to make sacrifices. Converting an idea to a business model and a business model to a viable operation requires time and attention beyond the norm.

New businesses are like new babies in that way: you must feed them constantly, day and night. I knew I was going to have to dial it up to succeed. But how could I possibly work any harder than I had already? The workload at the agency had almost landed me in the Montmartre morgue. Ambition and overwork had made me drift away from my values. Would I be replicating those conditions going out on my own? And what about the addition of a newborn to an already busy household? That's when it dawned on me. We were having twins—a baby and a business. What was I thinking?

PARTY TIME

It was customary to hold a short cocktail party for a departing senior staff member the day they left the agency. My party was in a function room at a hotel across the street. My boss and another colleague were my escorts through the underground passage that connected our building to the hotel. I was as somber as they were jovial. They were obviously happy to be seeing me off. I had planned many such wakes for departing colleagues, so I knew the next hour would be an ordeal.

We made our way up in the elevator to the second floor. I could have easily walked blindfolded to the function room, we had used it so often to dispatch people. As I entered the party, I heard my boss, behind me, shout: "Here's Judas!" Looking around the room at the faces of my colleagues, I could see some were in on the joke. Others, the decent ones, looked away in embarrassment. I, however, failed to spot a savior. The rest of the hour was downhill from there. I stood alone with a glass of wine, shunned, but despite the awkwardness, it was perfect. This charming departure party confirmed I had made the right decision. No matter what uncertainties were ahead, and I knew in my bones there would be difficult challenges, they could not be worse than remaining at the agency.

When the party hour was up, I left unnoticed and went back through the tunnel to my office. Supervised by the office manager, I took my two boxes of personal items and went down the elevator for the last time. At the back door to the building, Lynne was waiting in the alleyway with the car. I loaded the boxes into the back seat and we drove away, free.

The Fool's Journey

Start a huge, foolish project, like Noah.

It makes absolutely no difference what people think of you.

RUMI

THERE'S A fool inside every entrepreneur. Only a fool would willingly leave the security of full-time employment for the vagaries of the entrepreneurial life. Only a fool would risk everything on an idea, a hunch, a premonition. Who but a fool would allow him or herself to be seized by a dream?

History is littered with fools. Thomas Edison endured a thousand failures to invent the light bulb. Henry Ford and Walt Disney were serial bankrupts. Einstein and Pasteur barely made it through school. Steve Jobs and Michael Dell didn't graduate college. By the standards of received wisdom, these giants were fools, their inventions little more than pipe dreams.

Even so, each of them was compelled to leap, and to do it without a safety net, guided by little more than the certainty of their vision. *Forbes* estimates that more than 500,000 businesses start up each month in the United States, and according to Bloomberg, approximately 80 percent of these new businesses fail within eighteen months.[1] But despite the likelihood of failure and the chorus of skeptics and scoffers, entrepreneurs foolishly persevere.

Whether or not I was a fool in the cosmic sense, I was certainly beginning to feel like one as I sat facing my prospective bankers across a restaurant table. They held my one-page start-up budget in their hands, and with it, my short-term financial future. "Where's the revenue projection?" the bald one with the military-style mustache asked.

"It's forthcoming," I replied nervously. "I'm just waiting on budget confirmation from a client." Mr. Mustache frowned, looked back at my budget, and frowned again.

Beside me sat Dan, an old college friend. He had been with the bank since we graduated, rising to a branch management position after a decade of service. Dan was a good friend. As teenagers, we had worked underground as hard rock miners in the Canadian North. It was a particularly dangerous summer job where a lot could go wrong and go wrong quickly. I trusted Dan with my life, and that sense of trust was one of the primary reasons I'd turned to him for help with getting a loan. His bank was my bank after all. They held my mortgage, my retirement investments, and a small savings account. Dan thought it would be a no-brainer to get a loan since I had collateral in the form of equity in the house. I needed a $10,000 start-up loan, a figure I had cobbled together by estimating salaries for Elinor and me along with minimal operating costs. It would keep us going for a couple of months. While I had not heard from Elinor since our first phone call, I remained hopeful. Maybe, if I prayed hard enough, a polar vortex would form over Edmonton and the snow and cold would drive her back east.

Across the table, the bankers' expressions indicated they were less than enthusiastic about a business that had no track record, no clients, and no plan. What I thought would be a formality was turning into an interrogation. Dan seemed a little surprised too. He was shifting uncomfortably in his seat while trying to reassure his colleagues my business was a safe bet. My answers to the banker's questions were not supporting Dan's thesis, though. The bankers were glancing at each other with questioning eyes.

"Mr. O'Neill," said the sharply dressed banker to my left, "you understand we want to help. But you have to help us get you that help."

I nodded nervously. What had I been thinking? How could I go into such an important meeting, a meeting that was critical to my financial viability, so unprepared?

Mr. Mustache was the bad cop. He looked the part. "What we need from you to get that help is a signed contract; a business plan that includes first-year projections, expenses, and a profit forecast; and a personal guarantee."

"That sounds like a reasonable request," I said, trying to smile and look professional. "Reasonable" if you ignored the fact that all I needed to do was win the freestyle account almost single-handed and defeat my former employer. The agency would throw big money, international expertise, and teams of people into their bid, along with all the venom the Cobra could manufacture.

Out on the sidewalk, Dan was reassuring. "They're just doing their job. Don't worry. I think you'll get the money. I'll get another meeting for you, but bring a business plan. And a signed contract."

"Anything else?" I said.

"Maybe your firstborn. Just in case."

A business plan and my firstborn I could deliver. I was less sure about a signed contract. Like a fool, I was so in love with the idea of my own business that I had forgotten to behave like a businessman. I got in my car feeling embarrassed and disoriented. Somehow the car seemed to pilot itself from the eastern suburbs back downtown, while I regretted, moaned, and fretted.

My friend Reinhold had lent me a temporary office in his redbrick Victorian townhouse in a rough part of the city's east end. Reinhold was a graphic designer. German-born, he was a meticulous, generous man, and his offices reflected it. He had renovated the three-story building with one eye on aesthetics and the other on maximizing efficiency, and it was the nicest building on the now-gentrified block. I had a desk in what was once a back bedroom. It was a narrow rectangular space with off-white walls, track lights, the original hardwood floors, and a small Juliet balcony facing an alley. A good place to watch the crackheads, Reinhold suggested.

"How did it go?" asked Reinhold, smiling.

"Not so well," I said. "I think I made a fool of myself and made my friend look bad."

"Oh," said Reinhold. "That doesn't sound like much fun. Did the bank buy you lunch at least?"

"No."

"Bummer. Well, bankers can be tough customers. I don't have an extra ten grand . . . but let me know if I can help," he said, retreating down the hallway.

"Can you lend me a computer?" I asked.

"Yes, I have an old Mac you can use," Reinhold called back from the staircase. It was abundantly clear to Reinhold, and it was dawning on me, that I was woefully underprepared for this adventure. But as foolish as I felt in that moment, I also felt a deep roiling in my gut: the sensation of pure exhilaration.

THE FOOL

In the Tarot, the Fool is the symbol of awakening. Angeles Arrien suggests the Fool "represents your ability to give birth to new forms from a place of courage, wonder and anticipation."[2]

If so, then every entrepreneur who attempts to bring something new to the world requires courage, the willingness to risk, and the ability to see new possibilities. It also demands enlightened naïveté. To achieve a state of enlightened naïveté we must suspend disbelief and look at the world with fresh eyes, the way a child might. Or, you guessed it, a fool.

The Rider-Waite Tarot deck depicts the Fool as a fearless, carefree young man. Looking skyward, he carries all his worldly belongings wrapped in cloth and tied to a stick. He steps toward a precipice, seemingly unaware of the danger, and a small dog jumps up beside him. In some versions of the Tarot, the dog pulls at his clothing, a reminder to stay grounded while dreaming.

The Fool travels light, carrying little baggage. He or she has renounced all attachments to convention—especially conventional thinking—a singular requirement for the journey of discovery. Free of the status quo, the Fool is able to regain the innocence necessary for fresh vision. Stripped down to the "irreducible core" of the authentic self and retaining only what is essential, the Fool looks into the future without the encumbrance of the past. He or she sees a future fixed only by the limits of imagination.

The entrepreneur, like the Fool, is driven by a vision of how things could be rather than how they are. Optimistic by nature, entrepreneurs believe that creativity and innovation are far more rewarding than upholding old forms and enabling the status quo. Theirs is a journey of disruption and transformation.

Entrepreneurs seek the risks and challenges of a creative life. They turn away from toiling in someone else's fields; instead, they find their own. Jason Steiner, writing for *Forbes*, suggests the motivation of the entrepreneur has more to do with the benefits of the journey and less to do with the outcome.

> Why do entrepreneurs do what they do and take such great risks? It seems clear that financial gain is not a sufficient explanation... The answer lies in what are becoming known as *extra-rational motivations*. Such motivations lie mainly in the psychological rewards of being an entrepreneur and include benefits derived from:
>
> - the thrill of competition
> - the desire for adventure
> - the joy of creation
> - the satisfaction of team building
> - the desire to achieve meaning in life.[3]

The Fool's precipice confronts every entrepreneur. In fact, it awaits all of those who allow their dreams rather than circumstances to lure them away from a life of certainty and comfort. They never know if the creative adventure will end in disaster or deliverance. This risk is the central tension at the heart of every entrepreneurial journey. Trusting themselves and their vision, they step forward into unknown territory gripped by "extra-rational motivation." Between happy ending and disaster are the tests of imagination and character. These are the tests and the peak experiences that all entrepreneurs relish, though they are difficult. Those who make the leap from the precipice are fools; those who land on their feet are entrepreneurs.

THE ASK

The client called. Would I like to pitch the freestyle account? Could I be ready in two weeks to present my proposal? Did I understand I would be pitching against the agency? In fairness, they should be given a shot to retain the business, he explained.

"Yes, yes, and yes." I heard myself say.

Holy smoke! Game on! But what to do about money? With the bank less than anxious to lend me ten grand and my last paycheck shrinking faster than I anticipated, I needed to find some quick cash to get my pitch together. I also needed to bring Elinor from Edmonton to Toronto, and her plane ticket would cost money I didn't have.

Lynne and I sat together at our small dining room table deliberating over the client's phone call. Dinner was finished, and the baby was in bed. Lynne was having the intermittent contractions of false labor. I felt like I was too. "Action absorbs anxiety," I said, more to myself than to Lynne. "I need to make two phone calls: one to get Elinor to come to Toronto, the second one to my father."

"Do you think Ellie will come?" Lynne asked.

"There's only one way to find out," I responded. "I'm going to call her now."

I dialed Elinor's number. She answered on the second ring. "It's me," I said. "We have two weeks to get a pitch together. You need to get on an airplane."

"Really? It's happening?"

"Yeah. When can you be here?" I asked.

"I have to talk to Tim. Just two weeks, though," she warned, hedging.

Elinor was coming. I knew she could not resist the chase of new business. She loved to hunt. I nodded to Lynne who was searching my face for a clue and gave her a thumbs-up.

"Let me know what time you can be here tomorrow. I'll pay for your ticket. This will be fun!" I told her.

"You're such a jerk."

"You're going to love Reinhold's," I informed her. "Lots of interesting characters on the street."

"I know that part of town. It's full of bums." She laughed. "You fit in perfectly!"

"See you tomorrow," I said. "Thanks." I hung up before she could finish protesting. One precipice crossed, one to go.

The second call was far more difficult. I had never asked my father for money—never wanted financial support from my parents. It was a matter of pride. I wanted to be my own man, make my own way in the world without asking for a handout. Ironically, I was willing to ask strangers for money, but when it came to my own parents I was conflicted.

I also didn't want to frighten them. I knew they were already worried about me. They could see how often I was irritable, exhausted, or preoccupied because of my job at the agency. But even though they were aware of the price agency life had exacted, I was sure they had reservations about the timing of my leap of faith. Knowing that I had another baby on the way, they surely would prefer a less dramatic solution to my career crisis.

I would ask my dad for three thousand dollars. It wasn't a lot really—about six thousand in today's dollars—but it wasn't a little either. I was worried about putting him on the spot; he might feel obliged to say yes. But what if he said no? Lynne stood beside me as I dialed the number, trying to listen along with me.

"Hi, Dad. Uh, how's it going?"

"Who's that calling?" my mother asked in the background.

"It's your son," my dad replied.

"Ask him how Lynne is feeling," she instructed. "And when are they coming out here? I want to see my granddaughter."

"When are you coming? Your mother wants to know."

"Soon, Dad, soon." Like all good children I was beginning to experience acid reflux.

"He says soon," my dad reported.

"Dad, I was wondering if you would be willing to make a small investment in my new business? I just need three thousand dollars to get me started."

He paused for a brief second. "I was expecting you to call," he said. "I'm glad you did. Frankly, I was worried you might not have enough to carry you through the transition. I've been read-ing up on small businesses, and the number one reason they fail is by running out of cash. We can't let that happen. Come out to the house tomorrow," he said. "I'll write you a check."

I hung up the phone, flooded with relief and gratitude. Lynne and I did a strange little victory dance, constrained by the size of the room, the size of the table, and the size of my very pregnant wife. We were nowhere near the end goal, but this felt like a reprieve. We were now two steps closer to viability.

The following evening, I arrived at my mom and dad's house, about a forty-five-minute drive from our home in the city. My parents were delighted to see us. We didn't talk about the money until the end of the visit. Discreetly, my dad gave me the check as we were walking out the door. "Good luck from the both of us," he said.

{ 13 }

The Good Samaritan

And, when you want something, all the universe

conspires in helping you to achieve it.

PAULO COELHO

"SOMEBODY FOUND the check."

It was my father on the phone. It was 7:30 a.m., and I was just about to leave for the office. "What do you mean?" I asked in confusion.

"The check I wrote you for three thousand dollars. Somebody found it."

"That's not possible. It's in my backpack."

"You might want to look," Dad said patiently.

I left the phone dangling by its cord and rushed down the narrow hallway. My backpack was on the floor beside the shoe tray.

I opened it and began rooting through the contents. Nothing. In desperation, I dumped the contents on the floor and began sorting. "It's gotta be here," I said under my breath.

Lynne appeared in her housecoat with Alannah. "What's wrong?"

"My dad's on the phone. He said someone found the check," I was searching through notebooks and opening side pockets. "Oh my God! He's right. It's gone." I rushed back to the phone. "Dad, it's not here!"

"That's what I said. A man phoned me last night. He has the check."

"How did he find you?" I tried to sound nonchalant, but I was spinning.

"My name's on the check, Pat," he said bluntly. "Got a pen? I'll give you the man's phone number."

Deflated, I waited until 9:00 a.m. to call the good Samaritan. A woman answered the phone. I introduced myself and stated my reason for calling. "My husband found your check," she informed me in a gruff voice.

"I know. That's why I'm calling."

"He's not here right now. Call back this afternoon."

I took the subway downtown, too preoccupied with the latest start-up calamity to take much notice of my surroundings. I walked from the subway past the boarding houses, doughnut shops, and shabby bars toward Reinhold's townhouse. I reflected on my recent round of troubles. Stress, sleep deprivation, money woes, and a lack of structured environment were taking their toll. I had to pull myself together and focus on securing the freestyle skiing account. The clock was ticking. Elinor would arrive later in the day from Edmonton. That would help, I told myself. We could really roll up our sleeves and begin pounding out the proposal document. It would be good, like old times. Despite the prospect of such strong support from Ellie, I couldn't shake the sense of foreboding growing like a funnel cloud.

INTERCESSION

Mythologist Joseph Campbell suggests help comes to the imperiled hero or heroine on the journey of transformation in the form of a protector. World mythology, fairy tales, and religious traditions all feature unexpected and supernatural intercessions. Campbell's list is comprehensive: he identifies the fairy godmother, guardian angel, Christian saint, and the guide, among others, as figures of guardianship and protection.

> What such a figure represents is the benign, protecting power of destiny... that though omnipotence may seem to be endangered by the threshold passages and life awakenings, protective power is always and ever present within the sanctuary of the heart and even immanent within, or just behind, the unfamiliar features of the world.[1]

However, there is one figure left out of Campbell's accounting. The good Samaritan fits neatly into this category but with a twist. One of Jesus's most famous—and in its day controversial—stories, the good Samaritan answers the question "Who is my neighbor?"

While traveling the Jericho road, a Jew was attacked by robbers, beaten, and left for dead. Unlike Theseus, who was more than a match for the robbers he met, this poor man was naïve about the perils of cross-country travel, unlucky, or both. A priest and then a Levite passed the crime scene without offering aid to the victim. Maybe they were like many of us: a little too busy, a little too frightened. Or perhaps they were concerned about liability issues.

Some time later, a Samaritan rode up on his donkey. It's important to know that the Jews and the Samaritans were not on friendly terms; in fact, they quite disliked each other. The Samaritans were viewed as pagan despite their adherence to Mosaic law. Both sides harbored sanctions against contact with the other, but rather than pass by, as might be expected, the

Samaritan showed compassion for the victim. He cleaned and bandaged his enemy's wounds, put the injured man on his own donkey, and delivered him to the care of a local innkeeper. The Samaritan paid the innkeeper for the man's health expenses and promised to return and pay any additional costs the victim might incur. "Which of these three do you think was a neighbor to the man who fell into the hands of robbers?" Jesus asked.

The obvious reply is, "The good Samaritan." But there is something to be learned from the traveler as well. He is the neighbor whose story we know least and whose lessons remain obscured by the Samaritan's heroics and the tale-teller's brevity. The traveler reminds us that in order to gain help, we must be willing to accept help, even if it comes from the "other." While it is unclear whether the traveler was capable of consent, we can assume that at some point, he knew his welfare was a result of the compassion of a Samaritan. What turmoil this must have caused! The enmity between Jews and Samaritans was every bit as toxic as the relationship between modern-day Israelis and Palestinians, Serbs and Muslims in Bosnia, and Catholics and Protestants in Northern Ireland.

Every assumption and belief about "the other" must have been turned upside down by the Samaritan's charity. It is one thing to gain succor from a benign super-friend—Merlin, Glinda, or St. Michael. It is something quite different to accept your enemy, as Campbell puts it, as your "initiatory priest."[2]

THE RIGHT THING

I finally reached my good Samaritan, the man with the check. I had scribbled the address where we would meet on a piece of paper, and I clutched it in my hand like a compass as I looked for the building. It was on a rough-and-tumble side street not too far from Reinhold's. This intersection was, according to the local newspaper, host to some of the most violent crimes in the whole city. The building looked like a movie set: it was a low-rise boarding house, run-down and menacing. There was no doorman, just a couple of toughs huddled by the mailboxes smoking something illegal.

I went in on high alert. The apartment was a walk-up on the third floor. The hallways were dimly lit, littered with shopping flyers, and smelled of fried food. I half expected to be set upon by someone or something lurking in the shadows. Apartment 307 was at the end of the windowless hall. As I knocked on the door, a big dog began to bark from inside the apartment.

"Wait a minute," said a muffled voice. I could hear someone walking toward the door. "Stay!" he commanded the unseen dog. I hoped I wasn't going to be mauled by Cerberus the Hellhound.

As the door opened, I was surprised to see a familiar face. He was one of the "crackheads" I had seen from my office window. He was a small man with longish hair and a scraggly goatee. He was wearing a black Guns N' Roses T-shirt, jeans, and cowboy boots. Behind him, looking at me with red-rimmed eyes, was a scraggly mutt. "You Patrick?" he asked.

"Yeah," I mumbled.

The man reached into his pocket and pulled out a cheap wallet. He opened the wallet and withdrew my dad's check. "Here ya go," he said.

"Thanks. Where did you find it?"

"I picked it up on Dundas Street. I was on my way home from work. You should be more careful."

"Yeah. I know. I feel bad." I said. "Here, I want you to have this." I handed him five twenty-dollar bills. "A finders' fee."

"Uh, thanks," he said and took the bills.

"What's your name?" I asked.

"Tony," he replied.

"Tony, thank you for returning the money. I'm starting a business and this was a loan—"

"Yeah, I know," he said interrupting. "Your father told me. He seems like a nice guy, a gentleman."

"He is both of those," I said. Suddenly it dawned on me that making that call came at a cost to him. "You would have had to make a long-distance call to reach my father," I said. "Sorry to put you to that expense."

"It was the right thing to do," he replied, looking momentarily puzzled. "You better cash that thing," Tony said, as he closed the door.

Reeling, I made my way down the three flights of stairs as quickly as I could manage. I needed to get some air. I passed the two thugs at the doorway again. On closer examination, they weren't really thugs at all. They were young men about eighteen or twenty years old, wearing Toronto Maple Leafs ball caps and the ubiquitous jean jackets. They were smoking, all right, but I noticed it wasn't a joint. They were smoking cigarettes. One of the young men nodded in my direction. "How's it goin'?" he said.

"I'm having a strange day," I offered.

GRATIFIED AND ASTONISHED

The right thing to do. I thought about that all the way back to Reinhold's townhouse. The right thing had never been my motivation at the agency. "What's in it for me?" was a more likely motto. I hadn't invented selfishness. The agency was already a shark tank when I joined. But I had not promoted healthy values there either. Oh, I had protected my own. Part of that was loyalty, and part was making sure my army was big enough to successfully guard the fort or stage an invasion. Looking out for the other guy, however, was not top of mind.

That wasn't how I wanted to build my own company. I wanted to find a way to create a win-win-win. How could I do the right thing for me, for my employees, and for my clients? In retrospect, it seems obvious, even commonplace, but at the time it was such a new idea it felt like a biblical deliverance. I didn't know if it was something I could accomplish, but I wanted to try.

Mark Twain is said to have observed: "Do the right thing. It will gratify some people and astonish the rest." I was both gratified and astonished by Tony's integrity. Here was a guy who went out of his way to be a good Samaritan. He retrieved a check from the street. He made a long-distance call to find the owner. He agreed to meet a stranger to return the check. His only motivation had been to do the right thing. While I was gratified and enthused by Tony's neighborliness, I was less inspired by my own presumptions. I had pegged my good Samaritan as an unemployed drug addict when I first saw him from my office. I assumed he was more likely to rob me than help me. The guys smoking out front had appeared menacing at first glance, but when I really looked they were nothing like my projection.

A vision was forming with greater and greater clarity in my mind's eye: I was a snob. I was the priest and the Levite who could pass a crime scene without offering aid to the victim. But I was also the victim. Like the traveler on the Jericho road, my vision of the world had been upended by a simple act of humanity from someone I had judged harshly. I was learning the hard way about the initiatory road. It was an initiation into expanded vision, past my fears, biases, and projections. It was also teaching me about respect and the ability to look again past my fixed perspectives.

I arrived at Reinhold's and made my way up the stairs to my third-floor office. Elinor was sitting in front of the old computer, smoking a cigarette. "It's about time you got here," she said. "Where have you been? I've been here over an hour!"

"You're not supposed to be smoking in here. Reinhold won't like it," I said, slumping down in the chair across the desk from her.

"Whatever," she replied butting out the cigarette. "You're a mess," she observed. "You're shaking."

"I'm not doing very well." I recounted the events of the past twenty-four hours.

"Holy cow!" she exclaimed. "Well, it turned out O K. Let's not dwell on spilt milk. We've got work to do." She began to pound away on the computer keyboard. "Whenever I lose something," she continued, "I just pray to St. Anthony. He finds everything." She lit another cigarette.

{ 14 }

The Disrupter
of Programs

What's up, doc?

BUGS BUNNY

"THEY'RE PARTNERING with a sports marketing consultancy," Elinor said as she hung up the phone at our shared desk. "They've got a couple of retired athletes on the pitch team." Elinor still had many friends and a back channel into the agency. It wasn't public knowledge that she was helping me. Not yet, at least.

"Shoot! I should have known the Cobra would pull out all the stops to keep the account." Buying expertise was an easy way to gain instant credibility with a client. "Anyone we know?"

"It's those two guys the agency was planning to buy last year. You know—the deal you helped kibosh."

Great. These two ex-athletes had convinced the agency ownership their athlete representation business was worth high six figures. They seemed to know their stuff and were great schmoozers, but they managed better up the chain of command than down. I had shared concerns about the quality of their work with the management team after the jocks had dragged their feet on a project I was leading, apparently more concerned about selling their business. My complaint had halted the negotiation process, and now they would want revenge.

"They may be jocks," I said more to convince myself than Elinor, "but we know more about this sport than they do."

"The Cobra knows the client CEO very well," Elinor replied. "And she is a mesmerizing presenter. You have to come up with something better and different if you're going to win."

"You mean we," I said.

Elinor didn't look up from the computer screen. "This is your business," she replied. "I'm just here for the pitch."

We had been working on the freestyle proposal for days, mapping out how the sponsorship program would work. It was slow going. Neither of us was computer literate; we were still far more comfortable on electric typewriters.

The pitch was pedestrian at best. The agency account team had all its past programs to draw upon, and now they had also brought in a pair of big guns, adversaries who would be unpredictable. It was just the kind of strategic game changer that had cemented the Cobra's reputation.

I paced behind the desk, hoping to spark some creative thoughts as Ellie typed out a document on Reinhold's old computer. "We've got to find something special, something that sets us apart," I said. "A big idea."

"Quit stomping around back there," Elinor said with irritation. "You're making me crazy."

"You know they'll come up with a showstopper," I said. "They always do."

Elinor paused at the keyboard. "Lets get the meat and potatoes down first. The stuff we have to do—the sports media campaign, the customer appreciation events, and the athlete profile builders. Then we can look for a game changer."

"Yeah . . . OK . . . good. Grind on, Elster." We worked for several more hours without a break. It was early evening and we were both exhausted. Elinor paused and lit a cigarette. Suddenly the computer screen flickered and went black.

"Oh my god! What the hell?" Elinor was frantically tapping the keyboard and pushing the "on" button.

"Get it back on!" I shouted.

"I can't. It's dead."

"Oh my God! Oh my God! Where's Reinhold?" I jumped out of my chair, shocked into action, and ran down the stairs to find my friend. He was still at his desk. "Reinhold, the computer crashed!"

"Oh my!" he said, as we ran back up. "That's not good. Not good at all. That's an old machine. I hope you backed everything up on a floppy disk?"

"What's a floppy disk?" I asked, the panic rolling over me like a wave. "Ellie, did you save onto a floppy disk?" Elinor did not respond. I felt myself leave my body and plummet into a void.

THE TRICKSTER

The Trickster is the archetypal mythic teacher of detachment. The Trickster appears as Coyote and Raven to Native Americans, Mercurius and Hermes to the Romans and Greeks, Loki to the Germanic tribes, and Krishna to Hindus, among others. Bugs Bunny, the staple of Saturday morning television for many children, is our contemporary addition to the pantheon.

The Trickster reveals where we have become stuck in old viewpoints, behavioral patterns, and the status quo. The Trickster shows how delusional our thinking is when we believe we are somehow in control of circumstances.

In their book *Synchronicity: Through the Eyes of Science, Myth and the Trickster*, Allan Combs and Mark Holland suggest, "In the mythologies of many peoples, the mythic figure who is the embodiment of the unexpected is the Trickster, who steps god-like through cracks and flaws in the ordered world or ordinary reality, bringing good luck and bad, profit and loss."[1]

Anarchy, mischief, and subversion are the means and the impact of this energy. The Trickster can be a destructive force: Campbell termed it "the destroyer of programs." But it is also a creative force, allowing new forms to emerge through "cracks and flaws," leading us to transform our perceptions of reality. It is difficult to see new possibilities when we are locked within the status quo. The Trickster frees us from such conventions and allows us to expand our worldview. The Trickster reminds us that transformation can happen from misadventure and mishap as easily as it can from the hero's journey.

We can meet change with rigidity and reactivity. Or we can embrace it with acceptance and good humor.

THE MYSTERY'S PLAN

"There are two plans for every day," goes an old saying, "my plan and the Mystery's plan." Elinor and I sat in silence across the desk from each other. My plan had crashed over an hour ago. Like Wildcat, my nose was out of joint. Reinhold had left for the evening. He had been unable to recover the document we lost. Days of work on the proposal were gone. Our presentation was just two days away.

"You're screwed," said Elinor.

"We're screwed," I replied.

"I'm just..."

"Here for the pitch," I said completing her sentence. I got up from the desk and started to pace. "I'm going to track him down and kill him."

"Who are you going to kill?" asked Elinor wearily.

"Steve Jobs. And then I will hunt down Steve Wozniak."

"Good luck with that. Before you take them out, don't you think you need to figure out how you're going to get this pitch back on the rails?" Elinor was always good with roles and priorities.

I needed to get some rest. "Exhaustion never produces good results," I replied. "Let's call it a day and come back early tomorrow morning."

"You'll get no argument from me," said Elinor. "This was a brutal day."

We packed up our things in silence and headed for the subway. Elinor's train ran north, mine ran west. We mumbled goodnight and trudged to our respective platforms. I could always tell when Elinor was afraid, and right now she was about as scared as I had ever seen her, though she tried to hide it. I knew, despite the tough talk, she was worried we wouldn't be ready in time. I was worried too. I had my whole life, and the life of my family, wrapped up in winning the account. Now the file was lost and there was precious little time to resurrect it.

The subway pulled up and stopped. The door opened and I entered the car. It was empty except for a pool of vomit on the floor. *A perfect ending to a perfect day,* I thought. The door closed and the train lurched into the subway tunnel.

{ 15 }

Epiphany

All miracles come from a change in vision.

BASQUE PROVERB

ARCHIMEDES MAY not have been the first person in history to exclaim "Eureka!" but he may be the only one to do so while running naked through the streets. The most famous mathematician of classical Greece, Archimedes is remembered for his prodigious problem-solving abilities.

King Hiero II asked Archimedes to determine if his crown was indeed pure gold as commissioned or whether his goldsmith was a crook. Hiero suspected the tradesman had secretly added silver and kept some of the gold for himself. Could Archimedes make the determination without damaging the royal object?

Archimedes probably worked up a sweat pondering the problem because eventually he made his way to the public baths. As he lowered himself into the bath, he noticed that his body displaced a volume of water—and the volume of water displaced was the same as the volume immersed. In a flash of insight, Archimedes saw a solution. He took the crown and compared the volume of water it displaced to that displaced by a bar of pure gold, solving the mystery of the crown's composition.[1] Whether the goldsmith was a crook has been lost to time, but I'm betting he wasn't so pleased with Archimedes's ingenuity.

It is highly likely Archimedes employed either progress monitoring theory or representational change theory to solve the puzzle. Progress monitoring theory requires gap analysis—analyzing the estimated distance between where you are and where you think you should be—to solve a puzzle. At some point, a "eureka" moment is said to occur when you conclude you can't solve a problem using your current model of thinking. You must choose to think differently and explore alternatives.[2]

Representational change theory requires that you expand your vision by removing the constraints placed on problem solving. This is also known as "thinking outside the box." By relaxing the constraints on problem solving, previously unavailable knowledge can be retrieved from your memory and applied to access a solution. Perhaps the solution to the golden crown problem required both problem-solving approaches?[3]

Unfortunately, neither theory was proving fruitful in my quest to turn the freestyle account pitch to gold. It was 4:30 a.m. Obsessed with the crashed computer and the looming deadline, I couldn't sleep. I decided to get up and take a bath, but no "eureka" moment happened—I didn't feel the slightest urge to run through the streets of Toronto in my birthday suit.

Deadline: there was a good word. In the absence of an Archimedes effect, it described my fate perfectly—dead, and with everything on the line. I submerged myself, displacing water onto the bathroom floor. How long could I hold my breath, I wondered? *Thirty . . . thirty-one . . . thirty-two.* I surfaced, gasping for breath. Lynne was standing at the foot of the tub. "Practicing for the Olympics?" she asked.

"Something like that."

"I thought so," she responded. "Drowning yourself in the bathtub is unbecoming."

"I wasn't drowning myself. I was thinking."

"You know it's the middle of the night?"

"Yes, I am aware of the time."

She turned and walked down the hall toward the baby's room. "You'll figure it out," she said. "You always do."

FUNCTIONAL FIXEDNESS

Functional fixedness is a classic barrier to problem solving.[4] According to Gestalt psychologist Karl Duncker, the human mind can become biased by familiarity. The more familiar or routine something becomes, the more fixed our perspectives. Duncker's candle problem is a classic example of how functional fixedness limits problem solving. The candle problem involves two candles, a box of thumbtacks, and a box of matches. You must figure out how to use only these items to mount the candles to a wall. Most people try to use the tacks to fix the candles to the wall surface, a solution that is as predictable as it is unsuccessful.

An alternate approach is using the matches to melt the bottoms of the candles and fasten them with hot wax to the matchbox. The matchbox, holding the candles, is then tacked to the wall. Ironically, this solution literally requires an out-of-the-box orientation. You would have to expand your vision to see the matchbox as both a container for the matches and a platform for the candles.

We needed to find a way to expand our vision of the sponsorship. We were way too focused on the tactical plan, the things we had to get done. What we were missing was the answer to the question: Beyond the sponsor and the athletes, why should anyone else care about this sport?

The next morning I was back on the subway platform, vision still functionally fixed, headed to the office. Ellie and I had agreed to meet at 8:00 a.m. I hoped she had gotten some sleep because I hadn't. I was still running through options in my mind, trying to figure out how to recover the lost program from the ashes. There might still be time to bang out some approximation of the material. Would it be as good? Probably not. At best, it would be an inferior version of an inferior proposal—candles unsuccessfully tacked to a wall.

We would be pitching the proposal to a panel. The client had already informed us he held just one vote. The panel included the client's boss, a wily executive vice-president who was a master game player and enjoyed matching wits with the Cobra. Why would he want to interrupt his fun and award the freestyle business to me?

Elinor was already at our shared desk. She was tapping away at the keys of an electric typewriter. "I'm not taking any chances with this one," she said by way of greeting. "I'm trying to get the basics down from memory. It's going O K; I actually remember more than I thought. We can clean up the grammar later."

I had picked up coffee for us from Starbucks. I placed her cup by the illegal ashtray, already partly filled with today's butts. Ellie didn't look up. She had that "woman-with-a-purpose-so-don't-even-think-of-interrupting-me" look. I slumped down into the other chair at the desk and let her whale away. Twenty minutes later she looked up from the clacking typewriter. "What's wrong with you?" she asked with a look of concern.

"Ever heard of functional fixedness?" I asked.

"Nope. What is it?"

"It's when you're so close to something you don't see it anymore. I think that's why we're struggling to bring a fresh perspective to the proposal. It's too familiar. We have to find a way to think outside the box."

"What do you suggest?" Elinor asked, lighting up a cigarette.

"A bigger box."

THE GORDIAN KNOT

Alexander the Great may not have been the mathematical equal of Archimedes, but he was a brilliant problem solver in his own right. In the year 333 BC, Alexander tried to solve the riddle of the Gordian knot, named for Gordias, the king of the Phrygians.

The throne of the Phrygians had been empty for some time. An oracle, likely high on gas emissions, declared that the next person to ride into the city of Telmissus on an oxcart should be crowned king. Enter Gordias, a lowly peasant. He proved to be the luckiest oxcart jockey of all time.

Gordias was anointed king and was succeeded eventually by his son, Midas.

Still in his pre-golden days, Midas offered his father's oxcart as a tribute to the gods. He fashioned an intricate knot, one that could not be untied, to bind the oxcart to a post for posterity. There the cart stood, until Alexander arrived.

Another oracle foresaw the knot being untied by a man who would go on to conqueror Asia. Alexander aspired to the job, so he drew his sword and severed the knot in a single blow. This bold stroke set a mythic standard for solving problems using unorthodox means. The Alexandrian solution, as it is now known, is one remedy for functional fixedness. It is a metaphor for cutting through to the heart of a problem by focusing on the desired result rather than the current problem. Since the rope ends were woven into the knot itself, they were effectively inaccessible. An orthodox, step-by-step approach defeated everyone who attempted to solve the knot's riddle.

The Alexandrian solution required ambition, charismatic authority, freedom from conventional thinking, and a sharp sword. The solution was to focus on freeing the oxcart, rather than untying the knot. This was both progress monitoring theory and representational change theory in action.

THE BIGGER BOX

"What do you mean by a bigger box?" Elinor asked.

"I don't really know. It's more of an intuition than an idea."

"Your intuitions are usually connected to something. Can you put more words to it?"

I thought hard about Elinor's question. We had developed a Socratic rapport over many years that had produced some breakthrough ideas on behalf of clients. "I wonder if we're solving the wrong problem," I reflected.

"You mean trying to win the business?" she asked turning away from the typewriter and focusing her full attention.

"No, we should be trying to win. That's a given. It's more to do with the sponsorship itself."

"OK," she said looking puzzled. "We created the program and won awards for it."

"That's all true. But there may be an expectation that makes us vulnerable."

"Vulnerable to the agency?" Elinor asked.

"No, with the client. If we deliver what they expect, we will disappoint them. The agency will probably bring a similar approach. After all, they'll be working from our template. That will provide no real differentiation, and that's a risk. If we're not going to be a fresh mount, why go through the hassle of changing horses? We have to take it to the next level."

"So that's what you mean by a bigger box." Elinor lit a cigarette. She paused to reflect. After a few moments, she continued. "Let's go back to first principles. When we brought this sport to the client, it was an undiscovered national treasure. The athletes were fun, smart, and eager to show what they could do. In a word: gorgeous."

"That's right," I said. "You saw that immediately when you were doing the sponsorship search. You fell in love with the kids and the sport. They had charisma."

"It was so exciting to watch," Elinor continued. "I couldn't believe it wasn't on anybody's radar screen yet. The speed, athleticism, and sheer craziness made it perfect for television. Those kids had all the makings of national heroes."

"Yeah, especially the aerial and mogul skiers," I added. "When they're bringing big air to those jumps you can't look and you can't look away. That's what makes them 'The Canadian Air Force.'"

Elinor nodded in agreement. "We focused on the kids to showcase the personality of a brand-new sport."

"A sport where our athletes were winning medals," I added. "They were on the podium every weekend in a country where even the hockey medals are no longer certain." The momentum of the conversation was building. There was finally some electricity in the room. Progress monitoring theory was working to advance problem solving.

"Winning medals!" Elinor exclaimed.

"Yes! Winning medals! That's it!" I shouted back. We both jumped up from the desk. "Brilliant!"

"It's the Olympics!"

"They're not buying a sponsorship," I exclaimed. "They're buying the birth of an Olympic sport, one where Canada can dominate!" Freestyle skiing would be a demonstration sport at the Calgary Olympics. It was always a crowd pleaser, and it would certainly be a shoo-in for full medal status at the games in Albertville, France, four years later.

"How did we miss this?" Elinor asked. "It was right in front of us!"

"That would be a six-year commitment by the client," I added. "Perfect for them . . ."

"And perfect for us," finished Elinor.

"Us?" I asked.

"I'll have to talk to my husband," Elinor said, with a wide smile.

"The Olympics. That's the bigger box," I reflected. "Interesting. Lynne mentioned the Games this morning."

"OK. We've got to rejig this proposal." Elinor tore the page she had been working on out of the typewriter and inserted a fresh one. She began typing furiously. By 2:00 a.m. we had completed a first draft. I knew after reading it through that we had something the first proposal lacked: a vision.

It was the framework for an unofficial Olympic sponsorship. By sponsoring the Canadian team and promoting the notion that freestyle skiing should be admitted to full Olympic status, the client was getting the games without having to pay millions for the Olympic rings. It was a sponsorship steal. The client's business was building materials. We would brand the initiative "A building company building an Olympic dream."

"I think it's solid," said Elinor as she finished riffling through the document. "Let's come back in the morning and clean it up."

"We have to be at the client's office at 3:00 p.m.," I said. "It will be a race to the finish. But we really need some rest if we're going to make a coherent presentation." The subway had closed an hour ago; I placed a phone call to the taxi company.

"Wow! We're high rollers again. Cabs 'n' all." Elinor grabbed her purse, and we walked down the stairs to the main floor. The cabs were at the door within five minutes.

"See you tomorrow. Thanks," I called to her as she opened the back door of the cab and got in. Then I stepped into my cab, gave the driver the address, and promptly fell asleep.

"We're here. Buddy?"

The interior light of the cab was on. The driver was peering at me in the rearview mirror.

"Sorry," I said groggily, reaching for my wallet. I paid him and made my way to the front door of the house. As quietly as possible, I unlocked the door and entered the narrow hallway. I slipped off my shoes and climbed the stairs to the second floor, past the baby's room, and headed directly to our bedroom. There was no light on, so I waited at the doorway for my eyes to adjust before entering. I didn't want to wake Lynne. Fully dressed, I crawled onto the bed.

Lynne stirred. "How'd it go?" she asked sleepily.

"I think we're there."

"I knew it. What time do you want to get up?"

"Seven."

THE RACE TO THE FINISH

I woke with a start, wide-eyed and disoriented. I grabbed the alarm clock from the nightstand and checked the time—6:50. I hadn't overslept, thank God.

Still in my clothes from the previous day, I trudged to the bathroom and turned on the shower. I disrobed and climbed in. Hot. I needed it hot, then cold to wake up. Showered, shaved, and dressed, I headed down the stairs to the kitchen. Alannah was eating her breakfast at her pint-sized table. "Hi, Bug," I said, kissing her on the head.

"I'm playing with Laura today," my daughter informed me. 'We're playing dolls."

"Sounds like fun."

Lynne was making breakfast. I poured myself a cup of coffee.

"You were up late," Lynne said.

"Yeah. But we cracked the code."

"Good. I knew you would. You've got a sprint ahead."

"Yes," I replied. "And very little rehearsal time."

"Eat this on the way." Lynne handed me a fried-egg sandwich. I kissed my wife, grabbed my knapsack, and headed downtown to Reinhold's office.

Elinor had not arrived yet. Settling down at the shared desk, I considered the best way to tackle the day ahead. We needed to pretty up the paper proposal, get enough copies made for each of the panelists, and rehearse our presentation. We might just make it.

Elinor arrived fifteen minutes later. "OK," she announced as she entered the room. "We are going to win this pitch. We have twelve hours' of work to do in six hours. I have a plan."

Elinor's outline for the day was a detailed schedule designed to maximize rehearsal time and minimize time wasted in producing presentation materials. Alexander the Great could have invaded Asia far more efficiently if Elinor had been there to run the campaign. By late morning we had the presentation overheads and leave-behind documents ready for the printers. An hour later, we were ready to rehearse.

"You need to sell them on the Olympics," she suggested. "I can do the boilerplate."

Our goal was a maximum of forty minutes of presentation. We knew from experience that people couldn't process much more information after that length of time. While the presentation was important, leaving time for the questions and answers afterward was critical.

"We need to quantify the return on investment," I suggested.

"Yes, especially in relation to their advertising spend," Elinor confirmed.

"But how do you calculate the magnitude of the return when you're investing in national pride?"

"That's priceless," Elinor affirmed.

"This is a once-in-a-lifetime opportunity," I asserted.

"You better make sure they know it."

"No pressure."

By early afternoon we were ready. Gathering the presentation slides and proposal documents, we left Reinhold's office and walked to the subway. We hopped onto the Yonge Street train and traveled north twenty minutes to the Sheppard stop. The client's office was in a building right across the street from the subway station.

"Good, we're early," Elinor observed. "Let's get a cup of coffee."

"There's a coffee shop in the client's building. C'mon."

Elinor and I found a table close to a window. We ordered coffee.

"How much time do we have?" Elinor asked. She didn't wear a watch.

"Thirty minutes," I replied.

"Wow!" exclaimed Elinor. "Look..." She was pointing out the window. The Cobra and her team from the agency were leaving the building. "Don't they look pleased with themselves?"

Indeed they did. The Cobra was beaming. The two sports marketing ringers and a couple of other account executives followed her. They were obviously sharing a good laugh.

"Hope all the laughter isn't at our expense." Elinor sighed.

It was deflating watching our competition depart from what had likely been a very good presentation to the panel.

"We can't let this derail us," I said. "We've got to trust our vision." We sat in silence for fifteen minutes, drinking our coffee. "Time to go, Ellie."

We gathered our things together and headed to the elevator. The client's office was on the eighteenth floor. "Take a deep breath," I said to Elinor, and pushed the button. The elevator doors closed.

We entered the reception area, checked in with the receptionist, and seated ourselves on a couch in the waiting room. A few minutes later, our client walked into the reception and said, "We're ready for you. Please come in." In place of his usual warmth was a professional formality. We followed him into the boardroom.

Five senior executives were seated, awaiting our presentation. We shook hands with each of the panel members and took our places at the table. Elinor opened her briefcase and handed a proposal document to each panelist. As she was doing this, I stood up and walked to the head of the table, turned on the overhead projector, and took out the presentation slides. My hand trembled slightly as I positioned the first slide on the projector screen. I took a deep breath and began.

"Gentlemen, we believe you have a unique opportunity to bring an Olympic gold medal home to Canada."

{ 16 }

Gold

I love to fly.

JEAN-LUC BRASSARD

CANADA'S JEAN-LUC Brassard waited in the start gate to begin his final freestyle ski run, a run for Olympic gold. He had come to the Winter Olympics in Lillehammer, Norway, on a mission. France's Edgar Grospiron had been the dominant force on the Freestyle Ski World Cup circuit until a knee injury forced him out of competition for the 1992–93 season. Brassard, a charismatic twenty-one-year-old Canadian racer, was happy to fill the void. He commanded the podium until Grospiron returned to competition with a vengeance. Late in the season, with the run-up to the Olympics, Grospiron was on fire, winning four of five World Cup events.

Now, everything hinged on this final run, a run Brassard had to win if he was to unseat his rival.

The freestyle account team had gathered in Toronto, along with our client, to watch the showdown between Grospiron and Brassard. We were seated at a custom-built circular table in a glass-walled meeting room, the command center of our four-thousand-square-foot brick-and-beam office. It was early morning in Canada, early afternoon in Lillehammer. We were serving a champagne breakfast, hoping for the first gold-medal victory in any skiing discipline in Canadian history.

Brassard and Grospiron had qualified first and second. It would be a match for the ages. Everyone in the room was nervous and excited.

Since winning the account, we had had a very productive five years. We had built the profile of the athletes and the sport of freestyle skiing across Canada. Jean-Luc Brassard had grown up in front of our eyes. He had transformed from a nice young kid from Valleyfield, Quebec, to a sports superstar.

Our client had won the Sports Marketer of the Year award twice. He was recognized as a leader on the Canadian marketing scene, and his company enjoyed a reputation as a major booster of amateur sport. He had sponsored individual athletes, including Brassard, and also sponsored the Canadian team and World Cup events in Canada and abroad. He had also been responsible for building a television audience for the sport in partnership with major Canadian broadcasters. His personal brand, and that of his company, had never been stronger. The account, managed by us, was a textbook model of sports sponsorship. It was win-win-win all the way.

My family and company had grown along with the freestyle account. April, my second daughter, was born shortly after we won the pitch. Ariana was born four years later. Lynne and I had sold our semidetached home for a profit and bought a larger family home.

Our client list had grown as well. We had added some large national and international clients in the sport, manufacturing, beverage, food, technology, and service sectors. We had also grown to ten full-time employees, with freelancers rounding out the account teams as necessary. It had been a ton of work, but it was good work, and it was finally paying off. A gold-medal victory for Canada would be a crowning achievement for us as well.

All eyes turned to the television screen as Edgar Grospiron entered the starting gate for his final run. Sergey Shupletsov, a Russian skier, held a tenuous early lead, one that was not expected to hold. Grospiron was a racer of supreme athleticism, with a confidence that bordered on cockiness. Fast and fluid on the bumps, he was roundly acknowledged as a technical genius.

We watched as he exploded from the starting gate and charged at the moguls with reckless abandon. It was classic Grospiron. He was holding nothing back as he did the obligatory two jumps at breakneck speed. The meeting room fell into a tense silence. We all held our breath, hoping Grospiron would make an error.

Grospiron finished with the fastest run of the day. Despite struggling with his form at the end, he put on an exhilarating performance full of his customary swagger. He would be hard to beat. It seemed Brassard would have to be perfect.

I thought about our own experience competing for the freestyle sponsorship business. I knew what it felt like to have your back against the wall, to put everything on the line for a dream. That was pressure—but nothing like the pressure of having a whole country's hopes riding on your shoulders.

As Jean-Luc Brassard entered the start gate for his final run, it felt like the air was sucked out of the meeting room. There was dead silence. He wore his trademark sun-yellow kneepads. The kneepads allowed the judges to observe how fluidly he took his turns and how well his legs absorbed the pounding. He looked focused and determined.

On cue, Brassard exploded from the gate. From the start it was clear Brassard was employing a different strategy than Grospiron. He was more precise in carving his turns, a little slower, under complete control. You could see his confidence as he made his famous "Cossack" move, a spread eagle followed by a full extension of his legs sideways while pushing his hands forward. His landing was perfect.

Brassard crossed the finish line and reacted as if he already knew the result, pumping his fists in anticipation of victory. The meeting room exploded in celebration.

Peter Judge, the Canadian team head coach, strode into the finish area, joining his jubilant skier. Together they waited for the judges' scores. As ever, Coach Judge's demeanor was cool and collected, but a slight smile played across his face, betraying his confidence in Brassard's performance.

A roar went up from the crowd as the scores were announced. Jean-Luc Brassard scored perfect 5.0s from all the judges, with the exception of the French judge. It was gold for Canada!

Our meeting room was in an uproar. There were handshakes and congratulatory hugs. I was still watching the television screen as Peter Judge handed Brassard a cellular telephone. The camera showed Jean-Luc with a big smile, bringing the phone to his ear. A moment later, the telephone in our meeting room rang. I walked over, picked it up, and handed it to our client. The room went silent. "It's for you," I said. "Long distance."

Epilogue

At critical junctures, outer trouble and the inner need to grow conspire

to set each of us on a path of awakening and initiation.

MICHAEL MEADE

THERE IS an old Taoist story about a rice farmer who obtains some horses when they become mud-bound in his field. Asked by his neighbor for a response to his good fortune, he replies, "Good news, bad news, who knows?"

The next day when his son attempts to ride one of the horses, he is thrown, breaking his leg. Again, the farmer is asked for comment: "Good news, bad news, who knows?"

The following week, a general arrives to conscript the son. When he discovers the lad is incapacitated, he leaves him behind. The farmer's response: "Good news, bad news, who knows?" Every entrepreneur would do well to adopt the farmer's philosophy. Life in a start-up is chaotic. You can react to everything that occurs and exhaust yourself riding an emotional roller coaster, or you can meet it all as a challenge that can help you grow.

The news cycle in my own journey was equally unpredictable.

Sometimes the good news seemed more terrifying than the bad. Good news, like an invitation to pitch a new client, could lead to high anxiety because everything was on the line.

Bad news, like losing a proposal document in a computer crash at deadline, could spur an elegant new solution.

The thing I learned about daily news is it demands that you grow—continuously. In essence, all circumstances are initiatory tests. They require you to summon your personal gifts and character qualities, the inner capital of every entrepreneur. As I look back at my initiation into being my own boss, ten lessons stand out. These lessons could only be learned in the heat of direct experience.

1. ANSWER THE CALL

My call to the entrepreneurial adventure was a convergence of inner forces and external circumstances. The conventional notion of success at the expense of my health and family proved to be an investment with ever-diminishing returns. The ruthless drive for more was making me miserable and a misery to others. That realization forced me to confront myself. I did not like the person I had become. Like Jonah, I vowed to change.

I struggled to keep the memory of my epiphany fresh in my mind. It was hard not to fall back into workaholic tendencies, or be overcome by the daily grind. Fortunately, the outer troubles at home and work created enough dissonance in my life that I could no longer afford to procrastinate. I needed to find my best self.

I can assure you that your best self is waiting for you too. It lies beyond the comfort zone, beyond what mythologist Joseph Campbell identified as the barriers—"walled in boredom, hard work, or 'culture.'"[1] The entrepreneur's mission is to break with the status quo, heed the call of adventure, and in doing so bring something new, better, or different into the world.

2. BEFRIEND RISK

Risk and uncertainty are the entrepreneur's constant companions. They teach you to "Be open to outcomes, not attached to outcome."[2] Those who thrive on the entrepreneur's journey learn to welcome risk and uncertainty, seeing these things as a rich loam that nourishes creativity and productivity. Entrepreneurs are willing to try things out, learn, and improve. They don't give up when there are setbacks and reversals. Failures are expected—even welcomed. A client once gave me advice that I have found helpful ever since. He said, "Fail early in the process. That way you can learn, course correct, and get back on track." That resiliency is the measure of every successful entrepreneur.

Will you befriend creative tension? Can you learn in public and in real time? Can you stay the course despite the hurdles and difficulties? Can you see risk as a means to grow? These are the questions that challenge every entrepreneur to continuously improve, and ultimately, to succeed. Despite what Yoda said, the truth is there is only "try."

3. TRUST YOURSELF

The first measure of trust for any entrepreneur is the firm belief you can do what you set out to do. Without that conviction, you will never be able to answer the call to adventure or thrive on the rigors of the journey.

Trust is a relentless teacher. Just when you feel you can trust yourself, a new challenge emerges. Each challenge met funds the personal confidence, knowledge, and experience to dream bigger and act with confidence.

Here's a paradox. It is not enough to trust yourself: you must also learn to trust others and circumstances. No one succeeds alone. You must bring others into your dream. There will be things you don't know or aren't good at. There will be times when you want to give up. Without those who helped me—Lynne, Elinor, Martin, my dad, my clients, Tony the good Samaritan—I would never have lasted through start-up. Nor would my business have survived for over thirty years. Strong relationships lead to sustainable businesses.

In *The Alchemist*, Paulo Coelho writes, "And, when you want something, all the universe conspires in helping you to achieve it."[3] No one succeeds without some luck. No, you can't bank on luck. But you should expect it, and trust it when it comes, especially if you are working hard to create it.

4. COMMIT

Approximately two years passed between the time I realized I was hopelessly lost to the day I started my business. That's called mission drift.

I realized I was procrastinating and needed to find a way to thwart inertia. My solution? I made a commitment. I vowed to be in business by my next birthday. I began to take self-help steps, steps that took me outside my comfort zone. I didn't have to have everything figured out. I just needed to take actions that moved me toward the goal of leaving my job and starting a company.

Momentum built from that moment on, momentum that accelerated with opportunities that come from working from a time frame toward a goal.

Eventually, I found myself leaving the agency, crossing the threshold into my new life. I felt a little wobbly at first, uncertain about how to proceed, but you cannot overstate the thrill and the terror of working without the safety net of an established organization. It's a little like getting out of prison after spending so long in there that the outside world—where there are no prescribed system, expectations, or role—looks like an alien planet. One step led to another, and before long I was walking, then running toward my goal.

It took me longer to arrive at my stated intention of leaving the PR business behind me forever. That would come later, a few years into being an entrepreneur. But simply by becoming my own boss, I managed to solve part of my problem and began to find my own way. That step was monumental to me and contributed to my sense of being the master of my own destiny.

5. PLACE MEANING BEFORE MONEY

One of the things I learned in the "belly of the whale" was that the pursuit of material wealth was not enough for me.

I was also through with being a "hit man." Hyping products and being a spin doctor was not what I wanted to do for a living. I saw the price I was paying written clearly on my face: I was growing more self-centered, hard-hearted, and ruthless by the day. In a recent TED talk, author Nigel Marsh said, "Often, people work long hard hours at jobs they hate, to earn money to buy things they don't need, to impress people they don't like."[4]

That was me. And it was delusional to believe I could turn that persona off at the doorway to my home. Human beings are permeable. Work leaks into your home life, and your home life leaks back into work.

Dysfunctional cultures, like the one at the agency, create dysfunctional norms, and those norms feed dysfunctional behaviors. While some people can rise above such a culture, I was not one of them. I could see how work was causing me to behave in less-than-becoming ways at home.

Like Theseus in the maze, the only way out was to go "forward and always down." For me that meant looking inward to rediscover my values and principles. From there, I could find my way back to what was most meaningful in my personal and professional life.

6. DEFEAT THE SELF-CRITIC

The toughest competitor you will face is your own self-critic. It seeks to undermine your confidence and make you hide from the hero's journey. Instead, it wants you to play it safe and stick with the status quo.

The robbers that Theseus confronted and defeated are representations of the epic battle for dominion over our thoughts. Theseus teaches us the art of mastering the self-critic by remembering some simple maneuvers. Stand up for yourself, use fair self-talk, don't allow self-doubt to sabotage your intentions, don't fall victim to self-abusive behaviors, and don't wait for validation from others to pursue your dreams.

The entrepreneur seeks to rise above the negative chatter of the mind by recognizing it for what it is: fear. Fear that we are not up to the challenge; fear that we will make a fatal error; fear we can't make it on our own merits.

Self-worth, with its components, self-love, self-trust, and self-respect, is our best ally in managing the self-critic. By feeding the mind a diet of positive self-talk based in the original medicine of our strengths and victories, we fund the resiliency necessary for success.

7. BE A FOOL

The Fool, in the Tarot, is an archetype associated with adventure, creativity, and the search for meaning. Every entrepreneur is driven by a vision of how things could be rather than how they currently are. The desire to invent something new requires a certain enlightened naïveté, the ability to see convention with "fresh eyes."

Breaking with convention is risky business. You may be seen as odd, reckless, even dangerous. And of course you are. The most dangerous people in the world are the ones who think and see for themselves! These people have the ability to disrupt assumptions, challenge sacred cows, and call the emperor naked. Elon Musk, Steve Jobs, Oprah Winfrey, and Sheryl Sandberg are all unconventional success stories.

8. ASK FOR HELP

Many leaders believe they have to know everything, be competent in all aspects of their business, and be omniscient. They are the ones doomed to failure.

It doesn't matter how smart or successful you are, at some point everyone needs help. You might be a great strategist but a lousy accountant. You might understand how customers think but fail to understand employees. You might be a terrific salesperson but poor at operations. Don't let pride get in your way. Ask for help. I needed to learn to ask for help . . . and to receive it when it came. Asking my parents for bridge financing was difficult but absolutely necessary to survival. Getting Elinor's expert management skills into the business made all the difference. My wife, Lynne, provided the moral support and wise counsel I needed to take on risk.

Sometimes the help you need comes in the unlikeliest ways and from the unlikeliest people. Mr. Mustache, the skeptical banker, appeared to threaten my business, but he was actually an ally. Without his challenging questions, I might not have paid sufficient attention to strategic planning. I never forgot that meeting, because it taught me the value and importance of a business plan.

Other people make you better. They help your business grow.

9. DISRUPT YOUR THINKING

Breakthroughs only occur when you turn your thoughts on their side and expand your point of view. It is easy to get trapped in conventional thinking and follow the herd. The mark of an entrepreneur is the ability to disrupt functional fixedness—the bias of familiarity—and create something new, better, and different.

Cutting through the Gordian knot of functional fixedness can only be achieved through heightened curiosity. How can you look at an opportunity or problem with fresh eyes?

One means is by progress monitoring, commonly known as gap analysis. Another is by representational change theory—removing the constraints on problem solving. Thinking outside the box is easier said than done, though. It requires patience, tenacity, and the ability to enjoy paradoxes and puzzles. This practice alone causes personal growth. Can you remain committed to solving a problem, with no guarantee of success, for as long as is required? And pay the rent? If so, you've got the right stuff for entrepreneurship.

My own eureka moment was a result of a catastrophe. Losing my conventional business proposal at the last minute provided the pressure I needed to look beyond my fixed perspectives and discover a much broader and deeper solution to my prospect's business needs. That insight reaped dividends for multiple stakeholders, myself included.

Don't accept conventional thinking. Always search for innovative ways to solve problems, knowing that the search for answers in the outer world will demand transformative changes in the inner world.

10. ENJOY YOUR FREEDOM

The best (and maybe most terrifying) thing about being your own boss is the freedom to choose. In your own business, you make the decisions about who, what, when, and how. You will always have stakeholders, and you will need to take their needs into account, but running your own business lets you take control of your own destiny and shape it through the power of choice.

You are also in command of the vision and values of your enterprise. You are not bound by the dictates—or the dysfunction—of someone else's corporate culture. You have the freedom to guide yourself and your business from within your own ethical framework. If you stick to those principles, you can face yourself in the mirror every day and be proud of who and what you are becoming.

You will have the freedom to succeed and fail on your own terms. While we all like success, sometimes it's the failures that reap the biggest rewards. If you are prudent, you will learn from your mistakes. I have made my fair share, and every other successful entrepreneur has too. Accepting the bad with the good and being adaptable gives you the ability to change continuously, which is critical for sustainability. Many businesses fail to adapt to market and social changes because they get overly attached to the formula for success they started out with. Such attachments block reinvention, and these businesses become fatalities. The freedom to choose bestows agility. You will need it, as I have, if you want to make your business grow over years, even decades.

THE ENCHANTMENT OF MYTH

In her book *Maps to Ecstasy: The Healing Power of Movement*, Gabrielle Roth writes:

> In many shamanic societies, if you came to a shaman or medicine person complaining of being disheartened, dispirited, or depressed, they would ask one of four questions: When did you stop dancing? When did you stop singing? When did you stop being enchanted by stories? When did you stop finding comfort

in the sweet territory of silence? Where we have stopped danc-
ing, singing, being enchanted by stories, or finding comfort in
silence is where we have experienced the loss of soul.[5]

The face I saw in the shaving mirror that day long ago was that
of a man who had stopped being enchanted with his own life
story. I had suffered soul loss. My choice to pursue power and
wealth had turned me into a Midas. This revelation was so disturbing that it ignited a quest, a mythic journey to recover that
lost self. I made a choice to leave the toxic environment of the
agency behind. I learned, as Robert Frost stated, "The only certain freedom's in departure."[6]

That decision was like a leap into the void. I had no guarantee of success. In fact, others saw it as an act of foolishness.
Despite my fears, it became mythic adventure that transformed
my "little, local life" into one filled with meaning and passion.
It was a rite of passage.

Every life is a hero's journey. Every life contains archetypal
patterns and passages that carry us from the conventions of the
known world to "the region of supernatural wonder" contained
within us.

My advice? Don't settle for less. Don't settle for a dispirited
life. Start a business. Go somewhere you have never been. Court
the unfamiliar. That is the best medicine I know, the best way to
come home to yourself. You can have a rebirth, like Jonah, and
can find the freedom you need to live a life of mythic proportions.

Afterword

The future enters into us, in order to transform itself

through us, long before it happens.

RAINER MARIA RILKE

IN ORDER to sustain itself, my business, now in its thirtieth year, had to change and improve. And so did I.

The business I run today—a management consultancy—does not provide advertising or public relations services. I was eventually able to free myself from the professional quagmire of a career I knew well but could no longer tolerate. Writing press releases and making media calls for a living made me miserable. My heart wasn't in it anymore. I felt called to serve people in a different way, to develop new methods and skills that made a tangible difference in how people lived and interacted.

Today, I advise international clients on how to grow personally and organizationally through times of change, challenge, and conflict.

That transformation began with a vivid dream, a death in the family, a significant business failure, and an urgent requirement to reinvent myself. The process of reinvention, fueled in equal measures by mystery and dire need, took me from my home in Toronto to the peace process in the Middle East and the townships of South Africa. Throughout all of it, I was out of my comfort zone and at my personal growth edge.

The premonition I had in my first self-help class with Martin Rutte—the possibility that maybe someday I could lead groups seeking to improve personally and professionally—became a reality. I learned to lead groups, learned to teach and mentor—all in real time and at the front of the room, without a safety net.

I was not an overnight sensation. I had my fair share of teaching disasters, client missteps, and business near-death experiences. But I never gave up.

These further adventures—and misadventures—will be explored in my next book, *Extraordinary Conversations*.

Notes

INTRODUCTION

1   Joseph Campbell, *The Hero with a Thousand Faces*, 3rd ed. (Novato, CA: New World Library, 2012).

2   Jean Houston, *The Possible Human*, 1st ed. (New York: Jeremy P. Tarcher/ Putnam, 1997).

CHAPTER 1: A CRISIS OF MEANING

1   Rachel Naomi Remen, *Kitchen Table Wisdom: Stories That Heal*, 10th ed. (New York: Riverhead Books, 2006), 149–50.

2   Edward L. Bernays, *Propaganda* (New York: Ig Publishing, 2004), 71–71.

3   Angeles Arrien, *The Four-Fold Way: Walking the Paths of the Warrior, Teacher, Healer, and Visionary* (San Francisco: HarperCollins Publishers, 1993), 50.

CHAPTER 2: A GREAT DARKNESS

1   C. S. Lewis, *A Grief Observed* (San Francisco: HarperCollins Publishers, 2001), 38.

2   Anthony Sampson, *Nelson Mandela: The Authorized Biography* (New York: Vintage, 2000), 252.

3   Gerald G. May, *The Dark Night of the Soul: A Psychiatrist Explores the Connection between Darkness and Spiritual Growth* (San Francisco: HarperOne, 2004), 4–5.

CHAPTER 3: THE JONAH LESSONS

1   Hermann Hesse, *Siddhartha*, trans. Hilda Rosner (Toronto: Bantam, 1982), 71–72.

2   Joseph Campbell and Bill Moyers, *The Power of Myth*, ed. Betty Sue Flowers (New York: Anchor Books, 1989), 147.

CHAPTER 5: THE LABYRINTH
1   Ami Ronnberg et al., *The Book of Symbols: Reflections on Archetypal Images* (Los Angeles: Taschen America, 2010), 174.
2   Ibid.

CHAPTER 6: THE MONSTER WITHIN
1   Albert Camus, *A Happy Death*, trans. Richard Howard (New York: Random House Inc., 1972), 36.

CHAPTER 7: DEFEATING THE SELF-CRITIC
1   Angeles Arrien, *The Tarot Handbook: Practical Applications of Ancient Visual Symbols* (New York: Jeremy P. Tarcher/Putnam, 1997), 273.
2   Angeles Arrien, *The Four-Fold Way: Walking the Paths of the Warrior, Teacher, Healer, and Visionary* (San Francisco: HarperCollins Publishers, 1993), 21.
3   Jane Austen, *Mansfield Park: With an Introduction, Contemporary Opinions, and Contemporary Criticism*, ed. Eleanor Bourg Donlon (San Francisco: Ignatius Press, 2010).

CHAPTER 8: UNCERTAINTY
1   Peter M. Senge, *The Fifth Discipline: The Art and Practice of the Learning Organization* (New York: Crown Publishing Group, 2006), 139–40.

CHAPTER 10: ESCAPE ARTIST
1   Bernard Shaw, *Androcles and the Lion: An Old Fable Renovated* (London: Penguin UK, 2006).

CHAPTER 11: DEPARTURE
1   James Boswell, *The Life of Samuel Johnson* (London: Wordsworth Editions, 2008).

CHAPTER 12: THE FOOL'S JOURNEY
1   Jason Nazar, "16 Surprising Statistics about Small Businesses," *Forbes*, September 9, 2013, http://www.forbes.com/sites/jasonnazar/2013/09/09/16-surprising-statistics-aboutsmall-businesses.
2   Angeles Arrien, *The Tarot Handbook: Practical Applications of Ancient Visual Symbols* (New York: Jeremy P. Tarcher/Putnam, 1997), 25.
3   Jason Steiner, "What Drives the Best Entrepreneurs? Hint: It's Not Money," *Forbes*, February 13, 2013, http://www.forbes.com/sites/groupthink/2013/02/13/what-drives-thebest-entrepreneurs-hint-its-not-money.

CHAPTER 13: THE GOOD SAMARITAN

1   Joseph Campbell, *The Hero with a Thousand Faces*, 3rd ed. (Novato, CA: New World Library, 2012), 59.

2   Ibid.

CHAPTER 14: THE DISRUPTER OF PROGRAMS

1   Allan Combs and Mark Holland, *Synchronicity: Through the Eyes of Science, Myth, and the Trickster*, 3rd ed. (New York: Da Capo Press, 2001), 82.

CHAPTER 15: EPIPHANY

1   "Fact or Fiction? Archimedes Coined the Term 'Eureka!' in the Bath," *Scientific American*, 2016, accessed November 18, 2016, https://www.scientificamerican.com/article/fact-or-fiction-archimede.

2   James N. MacGregor, Thomas C. Ormerod, and Edward P. Chronicle, "Information Processing and Insight: A Process Model of Performance on the Nine-Dot and Related Problems," *Journal of Experimental Psychology: Learning, Memory, and Cognition* 27, no. 1 (2001):176–201 doi: 10.1037//0278-7393.27.1.176.

3   Günther Knoblich, Stellan Ohlsson, and Gary E. Raney, "An Eye Movement Study of Insight Problem Solving," *Memory & Cognition* 29, no. 7 (October 2001)): 1000–1009, doi:10.3758/bf03195762.

4   James Smith, *Managing Creativity: What You Need to Know: Definitions, Best Practices, Benefits and Practical Solutions* (Wahroonga, Australia: Tebbo, 2011).

EPILOGUE

1   Joseph Campbell, *The Hero with a Thousand Faces*, 3rd ed. (Novato, CA: New World Library, 2012), 49.

2   Angeles Arrien, *The Four-Fold Way: Walking the Paths of the Warrior, Teacher, Healer, and Visionary* (San Francisco: HarperCollins Publishers, 1993), 8.

3   Paulo Coelho, *The Alchemist: A Fable about Following Your Dream*, trans. Alan R. Clarke (San Francisco: HarperCollins Publishers, 2006), 22.

4   Nigel Marsh, "How to Make Work-Life Balance Work," February 7, 2011, posted October 25, 2016, https://www.ted.com/talks /nigel_marsh_how_to_make_work_life_balance_work?language=en.

5   Gabrielle Roth and John Loudon, *Maps to Ecstasy: The Healing Power of Movement* (Novato, CA: New World Library, 1998), xv.

6   Robert Frost, *The Poetry of Robert Frost: The Collected Poems, Complete and Unabridged*, ed. Edward Connery C. Lathem (New York: Henry Holt & Company, 1969), 460.

Bibliography

Ali, Abdullah Yusuf. *The Meaning of the Holy Qur'an*. Beltsville, MD: Amana Publications, 1998.

Archive for Research in Archetypal Symbolism. *The Book of Symbols: Reflections on Archetypal Images*. Los Angeles: Taschen America, 2010.

Arrien, Angeles. *The Four-Fold Way: Walking the Paths of the Warrior, Teacher, Healer, and Visionary*. San Francisco: HarperCollins Publishers, 1993.

—. *The Nine Muses*. 1st ed. New York: J. P. Tarcher/Putnam, 2000.

—. *The Second Half of Life: Opening the Eight Gates of Wisdom*. Boulder, CO: Sounds True, 2007.

—. *The Tarot Handbook: Practical Applications of Ancient Visual Symbols*. New York: Jeremy P. Tarcher/Putnam, 1997.

Austen, Jane. *Mansfield Park: With an Introduction, Contemporary Opinions, and Contemporary Criticism*. Edited by Eleanor Bourg Donlon. San Francisco: Ignatius Press, 2010.

Bernays, Edward L. *Propaganda*. New York: Ig Publishing, 2004.

Biello, David. "Fact or Fiction? Archimedes Coined the Term 'Eureka!' in the Bath." *Scientific American*. 2016. https://www.scientificamerican.com/article /fact-or-fiction-archimede.

Boswell, James. *The Life of Samuel Johnson*. London: Wordsworth Editions, 2008.

Campbell, Joseph. *The Hero with a Thousand Faces*. 3rd ed. Novato, CA: New World Library, 2012.

Campbell, Joseph, and Bill Moyers. *The Power of Myth*. Edited by Betty Sue Flowers. New York: Anchor Books, 1989.

Camus, Albert. *A Happy Death*. Translated by Richard Howard. New York: Random House Inc., 1972.

Coelho, Paulo. *The Alchemist: A Fable about Following Your Dream.* Translated by Alan R. Clarke. San Francisco: HarperCollins Publishers, 2006.

Combs, Allan, and Mark Holland. *Synchronicity: Through the Eyes of Science, Myth, and the Trickster.* 3rd ed. New York: Da Capo Press, 2001.

Eco, Umberto. *The Name of the Rose.* Boston: Houghton Mifflin Harcourt, 2014.

Frost, Robert. *The Poetry of Robert Frost: The Collected Poems, Complete and Unabridged.* Edited by Edward Connery C. Lathem. New York: Henry Holt & Company, 1969.

Gualco, Dean. *The Meaning of Life.* New York: iUniverse.com, 2005.

Hesse, Hermann. *Siddhartha.* Translated by Hilda Rosner. Toronto: Bantam, 1982.

Houston, Jean. *The Possible Human.* 1st ed. New York: Jeremy P. Tarcher/Putnam, 1997.

Knoblich, Günther, Stellan Ohlsson, and Gary E. Raney. 2001. "An Eye Movement Study of Insight Problem Solving." *Memory & Cognition* 29 (7): 1000–1009, doi:10.3758/bf03195762.

Lao Tzu. *Tao Te Ching.* Translated by Charles Muller. New York: Barnes & Noble Classics, 2013.

Lewis, C. S. *A Grief Observed.* San Francisco: HarperCollins Publishers, 2001.

MacGregor, James N., Thomas C. Ormerod, and Edward P. Chronicle. "Information Processing and Insight: A Process Model of Performance on the Nine-Dot and Related Problems." *Journal of Experimental Psychology: Learning, Memory, and Cognition* 27, no. 1 (2001): 176–201, doi:10.1037//0278-7393.27.1.176.

Marsh, Nigel. "How to Make Work-Life Balance Work." February 7, 2011. https://www.ted.com/talks/nigel_marsh_how_to_make_work_life_balance_work?language=en.

May, Gerald G. *The Dark Night of the Soul: A Psychiatrist Explores the Connection Between Darkness and Spiritual Growth.* San Francisco: HarperOne, 2004.

Nazar, Jason. "16 Surprising Statistics about Small Businesses." *Forbes.* September 9, 2013. http://www.forbes.com/sites/jasonnazar/2013/09/09/16-surprising-statistics-about-small-businesses.

Quora. "How Many Startups Are Created in the US and Worldwide Each Year?" 2017. https://www.quora.com/How-many-startups-are-created-in-the-US-and-worldwide-each-year.

Remen, Rachel Naomi. *Kitchen Table Wisdom: Stories That Heal.* 10th ed. New York: Riverhead Books, 2006.

Roth, Gabrielle. *Maps to Ecstasy: A Healing Journey for the Untamed Spirit.* Novato, CA: New World Library, 1998.

Sampson, Anthony. *Nelson Mandela: The Authorized Biography.* New York: Vintage, 2000.

Senge, Peter M. *The Fifth Discipline: The Art and Practice of the Learning Organization.* New York: Crown Publishing Group, 2006.

Shaw, Bernard. *Androcles and the Lion: An Old Fable Renovated*. London: Penguin UK, 2006.

Smith, James. *Managing Creativity: What You Need to Know: Definitions, Best Practices, Benefits and Practical Solutions*. Wahroonga, Australia: Tebbo, 2011.

Steiner, Jason. "What Drives the Best Entrepreneurs? Hint: It's Not Money." *Forbes*. February 13, 2013. http://www.forbes.com/sites/groupthink /2013/02/13/what-drives-the-best-entrepreneurs-hint-its-not-money.

About the Author

PATRICK O'NEILL leads Extraordinary Conversations Inc., a Toronto-based management consulting firm founded in 1988. The firm specializes in change management, leadership development, team performance, organizational communications, and conflict resolution.

A gifted teacher, consultant, mediator, and mentor, Patrick has worked with thousands of people and hundreds of teams and organizations over thirty years. He has contributed to the practices of leadership and wise governance by developing leading-edge organizational effectiveness programs that are practical, pragmatic, and applicable to the workplace and community.

Patrick's expertise in organizational dynamics has taken him to global corporations in North America, Europe, and Asia-Pacific; to the townships of South Africa; and to the peace process in the Middle East.

His corporate clients have included the Boeing Company, Teva Pharmaceuticals, the Ontario Pension Board, CIBC World Markets, the Walt Disney Company, Saab, Kraft, Nestlé, Pearson, Revlon, Telus, and Sony BMG Music as well as midsized and smaller organizations.

Patrick was a volunteer board member of the Angeles Arrien Foundation for Cross-Cultural Education and Research, a nonprofit charitable organization based in San Francisco. He is also a past president of the Learning Disabilities Association of Ontario. Currently, he is a volunteer advisor to War Child Canada, Pathways to Education, and the Adrian Dominican Sisters. He is also an advisor to Ryerson University's Certificate in Ethics program. Patrick's insights on leadership are regularly featured in national newspapers like the *Globe and Mail*. He is also the author of *A Hundred Chances: Short Meditations on Opportunity, Risk and Probability*.

CPSIA information can be obtained
at www.ICGtesting.com
Printed in the USA
LVOW03s0043290318
571576LV00001B/163/P